When
Push Comes to Shove

SUNY series in Violence
David F. Luckenbill, Editor

When
Push Comes to Shove

A Routine Conflict
Approach to
Violence

Leslie W. Kennedy
David R. Forde

State University of New York Press

Published by
State University of New York Press, Albany

© 1999 State University of New York

For information, address State University of New York
Press, State University Plaza, Albany, N.Y., 12246

Production by E. Moore
Marketing by Patrick Durocher

Library of Congress Cataloging-in-Publication Data

Kennedy, Leslie W.
    When push comes to shove : a routine conflict approach to violence
/ Leslie W. Kennedy and David R. Forde.
        p.   cm. — (SUNY series in violence)
    Includes bibliographical references and index.
    ISBN 0-7914-4033-8 (hc : alk. paper). — ISBN 0-7914-4034-6 (pbk.
: alk. paper)
    1. Violence—United States. 2. Interpersonal conflict—United
States. 3. Social conflict—United States. 4. Aggressiveness
(Psychology)—United States. I. Kennedy, Leslie W. II. Forde,
David Robert, 1959–   . III. Title. IV. Series.
HN79.V5K45 1998
303.6′0973—dc21   98-10496
                                                                        CIP

10 9 8 7 6 5 4 3 2 1

To Ilona, Alexis, Andrea, and grandparents

To my parents, Bill and Sally Forde

Contents

Tables and Figures

Tables

Figures

Preface

In the early 1990s, *On the Borders of Crime* was published. This book reviewed the relationship between social conflict and crime. Using the arguments put forward there as a starting point, we set out to empirically test the way in which crime, in general, and violence, in particular, connects to ongoing daily social conflict. We were fortunate to receive funding from the Social Sciences and Humanities Research Council to conduct a large survey in two Canadian provinces and to pay for data processing for a street study conducted by Stephen Baron. The products of these studies are the focus of this book.

The revelation in recent years that violence is connected with all parts of life (public and private) and the realization that mainstream society tolerates many forms of violence leads us to inquire, under what circumstances do people use or resist the use of violent means in solving everyday disputes? We are pleased to have the opportunity in this series to explore these issues in great detail and hope that you, the reader, are left with new insights about violent ways and violent situations.

We would like to thank our editor Zina Lawrence; David Luckenbill, Northern Illinois University, editor of the series; and the editorial review committee at the State University of New York (SUNY) Press for their ongoing support for this project.

Les Kennedy would like to thank colleagues and students at the University of Alberta, in particular Mike Gulayets, Erin Van Brunschot, Laura Thue, Fiona Gironella, and Hannah Scott for their comments and feedback on the manuscript. Kerri Calvert provided outstanding assistance in finding material for the book. Also, Cliff Kinzel, Fran Russell, and Kelly McGuirk Petryk were instrumental in ensuring that the survey component of the study was successfully completed. Once again, Andrea, Alexis, and Ilona showed great patience while he labored over yet another book.

David Forde would like to thank David Giacopassi and Marianne Bell for their comments on the manuscript. Russell Smandych, Candace Reinsch, and Jyoti Grewal helped in the preparation of this project. Charliene Havixbeck and Tracey Lewis were patient and dedicated in coordinating this survey, along with the Winnipeg Area Study. Last, I would like to thank Raymond Currie, founding director of the Winnipeg Area Study, for his mentorship and research support while I was at the University of Manitoba from 1991 to 1994.

Chapter 1

Violence in Everyday Life

J effery Farina, when asked why he shot three people and stabbed another
in a fast food store in 1992, replied that he had had a boring day. Farina,
on death row in Florida for the murder of one of the persons who died as
a result of the wounds he inflicted that day, has been described as a typical
"stone killer." Stone killers murder with no apparent motive. The crimes they
commit are preceded by what appear as trivial events (an insult or accidental
nudge), or by no apparent stimulus at all. The unimportant nature of the interaction preceding the attacks is further underlined by the explanations for their
behavior, offered by offenders such as Farina. When asked why he acted in
such a violent way, the stone killer responded with shrugs or laughter, suggesting that the fatal event served up a moment of entertainment in his otherwise uneventful life (Sataline 1994).

Stone killers frighten us. They epitomize the central reason why people
are so fearful of crime, that is, the threat of random violence at the hands of
strangers, who act for no apparent reason other than for kicks. Society looks
on these individuals with particular horror, despite the fact that stone killers
seem to be rare and their murders no more or less grizzly than those of others.
Their lack of rationale, their inability to point to any specific cause (or they
suggest a cause that appears trivial) for becoming violent, makes them appear
more dangerous and threatening than those who can offer specific reasons
why they act this way. The media ask, "What makes cold-blooded killers do
what they do?" This question itself suggests that despite the caricature of
these individuals operating without feeling or motive, reinforced by vacant
stares and mindless shrugs when asked to answer this question, we find it hard

to believe that there is no reason for them to act violently. Further, the stone killer scares us in part in that it challenges our belief that there should be something we can do to stop people from acting in such destructive ways. We expect that people will conform and follow orderly and nonharmful behavior because they value other peoples' lives. But, if not, we would like to believe that others' actions can deter potential offenders from committing their fatal acts.

Are stone killers real? Stone killers may, in fact, be more realistically viewed as a construction of an overly excitable media that hangs on the words of barely articulate juveniles, as though these are a true expression of their innermost feelings. James Gilligan, a psychiatrist who has worked extensively with violent offenders, questions the assumption that many people kill for no reason. As he explains, much criminal violence derives from a desire on the part of offenders for justice or revenge (Gilligan 1992). Gilligan begins his analysis with the assumption that in their efforts to reduce shame or humiliation, individuals become violent as a way of projecting their own selves and promoting their own self-esteem. As he states, ". . . a man only kills another when he is, as he sees it, fighting to save himself, his own self. . . murderers see themselves as having no other choice; to them, 'it's him or me' (or 'her or me')." This reduction of choices, Gilligan argues, should not be confused with the triviality of the incident that provokes or precipitates the efforts to reduce shame. While the incident that triggers the violence may seem unimportant or mundane, it may be the last straw for individuals who feel that they have suffered a long series of insults.

This view of violence suggests that there are reasons for violence that go beyond the poorly articulated explanations of specific events. Beyond the reactions to shame, individuals also may use violence to control or punish others—to coerce them to act in certain ways. But, again, the "motive" for this violence may not be clearly understood if we look only at the explanations offered by the offender.

Gilligan points out that most people do not commit any acts of significant violence in their entire lives. He suggests that most people have available to them a nonviolent means to protect or restore their wounded self-esteem, or else the circumstances in which they find themselves make it difficult for them to accomplish, through violence, their needs. Beyond that, Gilligan suggests, most people possess the capacity for guilt and empathy for others that will not permit them to engage in lethal violence, except under extraordinary conditions (p. 114). Gilligan also points out that even the most violent people on earth, those who assault and kill, are not violent most of the time. They are violent in brief, acute crises.

Gilligan draws upon the literature from the medical and biological sciences to formulate explanations for these crises and the violence. Yet the concepts he defines as being important for explaining violence—shame, self-esteem, social circumstance, guilt, and choice—are more a product of social interaction than of disease. Injustice and revenge evolve from social learning and community values. Gilligan works in a clinical setting that demands the assessment and treatment of individual offenders to deter their antisocial behavior. Also, he has as his focus the most violent of offenders, those who are incarcerated for murder and serious assault. But what about violence in the general population, where treatment does not consist of drug therapy or conditioning programs but of parental guidance and socialization in school? The broad-based occurrence of violence in society suggests that we need to go beyond the offender for our explanations and look at violence as it viewed by the total population. We must look for resolution in low-intensity situations, as these events may socialize or resocialize individuals in developing alternative ways to deal with their problems.

In the discussion that follows, we will pursue an explanation of the social roots of violence by using an approach that attends both to low-intensity and high-intensity conflict originating from social interaction. We begin with similar assumptions to those of Gilligan's. If people act violently, we believe that this can be explained by circumstances surrounding the event; previous relationships; and/or the presence of drugs or alcohol. Violent offenses may emerge from interactions gone sour, may develop from a desire to coerce others or punish them. Violence may be due to anger or frustration. These outcomes derive from the constant ongoing interaction in which people involve themselves on a daily basis. The rules or conventions that govern these interactions may include choices that preclude violent or aggressive action. Alternatively, the choices people exercise may be so limited that violence seems to be a reasonable option in resolving certain types of conflict.

The Routinized Nature of Violence

The everyday aspects of daily life that offer constraints and choice related to aggression and violence are a major focus of the discussion in this book. An important element of our approach to violence is the view that these actions emerge from normal nonviolent interaction. Given this view, it should not be surprising that we would argue that this interaction is based on basic routines people use to help them navigate through daily living. It is clear that we do not go through life making up new forms of interaction with each person we encounter. These conventions and rules are offered to us in socialization and are tried out over time. Mostly, the successful conventions are retained and routinized, and the less successful conventions are discarded. Sometimes, though, people retain destructive routines or are faced with situations in which the only options they see available are routines that are harmful to others.

For example, there has been a great deal of attention focused on recent judicial decisions concerning the culpability of women who have killed their husbands after a long history of victimization from spousal violence. In many cases, women who have acted in this way have struck out at their husbands in what appears to be a nonprovoked fashion, sometimes shooting them in the back or while they were asleep (Silverman and Kennedy 1993). The justice system has previously treated this as evidence not of self-defense but of premeditated murder. Recently, though, there have been major changes in the way in which courts have come to look at these murders. Rather than accepting a limited definition of self-defense, there have been cases in which the courts have ruled that the homicidal act cannot be considered outside of the total interaction that occurred between the couple over some period of time.

In accepting the idea of the "battered women defense," courts have said that the ongoing battering a woman has experienced can have the effect of creating in her mind a sense of danger, even when she is not imminently being provoked or threatened by her partner. This perception of the battered woman can lead to intense fear and to the conclusion that the only option available to save her own life is to kill her antagonist. In accepting this claim, the courts have acknowledged a broader definition of what constitutes the definition of culpability. They have accepted a wider time frame in which social interaction that leads to violent outcomes can be considered, and they have accepted that individuals who choose to be violent may do so only because they feel they have no other recourse.

Choices may be based on lessons learned from watching others deal with stressful situations, as in cases of children who witness family violence and then exercise the same harmful actions on their spouses or children (Widom 1989, 1995). This link between seeing others resolve disputes in a violent way and the use of these techniques in resolving one's own conflicts seems fairly obvious. But recent research on the cycle of violence provides a more ominous perspective on this problem. Of children who had histories of abuse and neglect, tracked over a twenty-five-year period, almost half had been arrested for some type of nontraffic offense and 18 percent had been arrested for a violent crime (National Institute of Justice 1996).

The high arrest rate among neglected children alerts us to the importance of not only the learning of poor conflict resolution tactics from experience with abuse but also the improper learning of nonviolent tactics through poor socialization that comes from neglect. There is increasing evidence that physically aggressive young children must be taught to learn other tactics to deal with their frustrations as they age (Tremblay et al. 1996). Through tactics that increase prosocial behavior and offer children ways in which they can channel aggression, we find that children's aggressive behavior can desist. These findings point to the importance of learning in the reduction of violent behavior.

Equally important to this equation is the extent to which children confront situations in which they feel threatened and expect little help from others. Highly oppressive environments, "oppositional cultures," promote aggressive responses and offer limited choices of how to resolve conflict. These environments have been described in field studies of inner-city gangs (Hagedorn 1994); street life of African Americans (Anderson 1994); the experiences of the poor (W.J. Wilson 1991) and the homeless (Jencks 1994).

Put together, children and adolescents who have experienced abuse and/or neglect and who live in oppositional environments have higher levels of aggression and use violence to a greater degree to solve their problems. Increases in violent behavior that we have witnessed in the past decade center on groups that fit this profile. It is the violence among young, dispossessed males that has become of greatest concern in our society. Crime committed by this group climbs inexorably, as crime for other groups begins to drop. There are predictions that this crime pattern will simply get worse as these young people increase in numbers, an inevitable consequence of the population explosion that is occurring in these disadvantaged populations (J.Q. Wilson 1994).

While this extreme violence is of concern to us here (and will be explored in our study of street youth, presented in chapter 7), there are elements in this picture that we can use to understand violence that occurs not only among the disadvantaged but also as it occurs in other sectors of society. We can see the genesis of elements of violence coming from the same roots, that is, the types of choices people make in the way they confront others in social interaction. We observe this while acknowledging that these choices come to be limited or altered by disadvantage, through neglect, or by abuse. It may be that individuals belong to a group in which violence is an acceptable (and possibly an encouraged) form of managing conflict. Street kids will express the opinion that violence is a normal part of life on the street, and they use it to get things they want or to protect themselves with great regularity (Kennedy and Baron 1993). Male batterers, on the other hand, can come from a broad spectrum of socioeconomic strata. Understanding how men use violence to exert power in relationships may be more important in these cases than knowing about the frustrations of poverty and disadvantage.

Whatever their origins, violent routines are more or less available to people based on what they have learned and on what they expect to happen in different situations. This is not to argue that violence is routine, but that it is routinized, following certain patterns that are common to particular groups of individuals, certain situations, and specific circumstances. The response sets that people develop, then, are viewed in the context of the point at which an interaction escalates from a simple disagreement to a violent encounter. Put another way, violence is a choice most people can consider but many do not exercise because of learning or external constraints.

Social Construction, Coercion, and the Criminal Event

There are times in which violence appears to be the preferred, or only, option for satisfactorily dealing with the other person with whom one is interacting, although in most cases in our society we would like to believe that we can deal with problems without having to use violence. In pushing people toward violence, there are three different aspects of the interaction that must be considered: the structure, process, and content of social events. Structure is addressed through a social constructionist approach. Process looks at the evolution of social events over time, and includes relationships between major parties involved, social circumstances, and the aftermath of the act. Content includes a consideration of the aspects of coercion that are included in violent acts.

First, in the social construction of behavior, individuals learn, in general terms, to structure what is acceptable and what is not in social interaction. We can see this construction operating at the level where rules and regulations are developed; norms are articulated and individuals are socialized; and punishments and restraints are developed in a set of guidelines that are used to control or constrain violent behavior. While this construction may not directly influence violent events, it has the effect of stating the terms under which interaction takes place and of determining what the consequences of certain types of actions will be. We cannot understand how people make choices unless we understand what these choices are and how they come to be defined in the society. This approach draws from literature on the sociology of law (Black 1983; Silbey and Sarat 1987), including the use of alternative justice approaches to react to and remediate conflict situations, even those that involve violence (Kennedy 1990; Merry and Silbey 1984).

Second, to understand violence, we need to see it as only one of a number of likely outcomes in social interaction. Erving Goffman (1974), in his book *Frame Analysis*, theorizes that conflict develops through the frame of experience, with individuals anticipating certain consequences from their actions based on previous contacts with others and with the cues gained from situational factors that surround interaction. Luckenbill and Doyle (1989) extend this theme in their discussion of the "situated transaction." They suggest that transactions are predictable, based on a convergence of structural conditions driving people to escalate conflicts toward aggression. Adding to the debate, Bernard (1990) offers the concept of "angry aggression," under-lining the role of predisposition that people bring to interaction based on past experience and expectations in raising levels of interpersonal aggressiveness.

We need to address not only the act of violence itself but also what pre-cedes and follows this violence (Miethe and Meier 1994; Sacco and Kennedy 1996). The precursors of the violent event include, among other things, the previous relationship of the combatants; whether the interaction is public or private; and the routines people have learned in handling social conflict. The transaction itself includes the actual act that takes place, including the action that leads to harm, the reactions to avoid this harm, and the behavior of other people who are present. The aftermath involves the reaction of others to the action; the intervention of authorities (sometimes involving arrest); the long-term harm; and the punishment of the offender. This approach assumes that all violent offenses, to be properly understood, must be looked at as a process that evolves over time and contains separate stages in this evolution.

The third component of our analysis, content, suggests that there are times in which violent action may be seen as a necessary response by an indi-vidual in social interaction. This action can be viewed as coercive, an act that is used by one person in an instrumental fashion toward another. Reasons to use coercion include saving face; retaliating for some other person's violence; punishing the other person; or trying to get someone else to do something for you (Tedeschi and Felson 1994). This perspective allows us to consider the content of the social interaction. Rather than looking only at the harm done or considering the impulsive nature of violent offenders, considering coercion forces us to look at the whole interaction. The relationship between offender and victim plays a decisive role in pressuring individuals to act in a certain way, depending on their interpretation of the situation and their views of how the others in the interaction are responding to their demands. Violence is one way of influencing others and getting one's way.

Our approach views most violence as being one possible outcome of a normal interaction rather than a product of maladjusted personality bent on wreaking havoc with others' lives. We can even go so far as to say that the actions of the stone killers and young men who assault one another in bars can be analyzed using a similar approach. There is no need to develop a special theory for homicide, for example. It makes more sense to see acts of violence on a continuum, where fatal actions represent an extremely harmful escalation of more mundane disagreements or coercive actions. The fact that one party ends up dead need not make us change our view of why these conflicts occur, although they clearly make our search for answers about how to curtail this escalation to violence much more urgent.

Support for this view comes from the research that confirms that a large majority of murders derive from arguments or disagreements between individuals who most often know one another prior to their fatal encounter (Silverman and Kennedy 1994). These results show up in official police statistics about victim and offender relationships and are also confirmed in interviews of offenders who report on the circumstances surrounding a killing (Luckenbill 1977). Confrontations between disputants may or may not result in fatal outcomes (and, of course, most do not end as a homicide), but many situations do escalate to violence where someone gets hurt. Assaultive behavior is the most common of all violent crime. The pervasiveness of interaction leads us to search for explanations of violence across the broad range of all conflict. From this we can draw an understanding of how the disruption of orderly interaction leads to aggression and harm.

The outcomes of interaction are not always predictable, however. A clear failure of police, the family, and the victim to anticipate a lethal outcome is evident in the example of the family that sought to sue the police for negligence when they did not arrest a man who had threatened his wife with a gun and later shot her. The police defended their inaction in dealing with the threats by arguing that this type of incident is so commonplace that the likelihood that the husband would kill his wife was negligible. They felt that the woman was safe. The fatal outcome, they suggested, was an unlikely outcome based on this couple's previous interaction and based on what they knew about others in similar circumstances. In retrospect, the police can be shown that the signs were clear that the woman was in danger and that her husband was likely to act in this way. The choices for police are limited, however, in what they can do in these circumstances. They can arrest the husband, and/or they can encourage the wife to seek help. But, they argue, they cannot provide around-the-clock protection to all people who are at risk. They hope that the conflict stays at a nonviolent level, and most of it does.

The point here is not simply that there was a failure to predict fatal outcomes (this seems impossible) but to understand the underlying forces that contribute to interpersonal conflict that may be harmful and then take steps to curtail it. While it is true that the police cannot lock up everyone, nor protect all potential victims of violence, they and other agencies can provide help to people who need to change the ways in which they interact. An important part of this matrix is addressing the social context in which social interaction takes place.

Social Context and Interaction

People have many different reasons for getting into conflict, as we will see in this book. Conflicts will vary by the nature of the relationship that they share with others; they may be public or private; they may involve a fight over money, sex, or drugs, or they may involve a trivial disagreement based on a perceived slight or a misunderstanding that leads to hostile gestures and quick anger. Conflicts may lead to threats or physical harm or a quick parting of combatants that cools off the conflict and avoids trouble. Conflicts may have long histories, where the combatants have been feuding for years, or they may spark between strangers who have never before met.

The broad range of possibilities for conflict is complemented by a wide selection of potential solutions to conflict. These vary from vague and messy disentanglements based on emotional responses to involvement of police who have guidelines[1] that they use to determine whether or not the actions require criminal sanction or should be dealt with in an informal manner. It is noteworthy that we know so little about how people actually develop routines to handle conflict or avoid becoming involved (as cither an offender or a victim) in violence. Is it because of the infrequent occurrence of these types of encounters or the fact that they develop so quickly that people are slow to respond to them with appropriate action? But is there more to this than slow reactions? The underlying reason for this lacuna in our understanding of this form of human behavior might rest in the aversion that people have in confronting the unsettling nature of conflict. Are we socialized to deal only with a limited number of situations that develop, leaving us unprepared to handle conflict that develops in unfamiliar circumstances under extreme conditions? Alternatively, are people who confront conflict, as prepared as they may be to handle the problems in certain ways, overcome with anger or frustration and act in impulsive ways to threatening situations? Is conflict an extraordinary part of human existence—unanticipated, hard to manage, emotional, and fraught with dangers, including violent outcomes?

While conflict may be all of these things, it seems implausible that this is behavior that is unanticipated in social interaction, particularly if we see it as an escalation from nonaggressive or nonviolent encounters. Also, it is apparent that conflict and violence are the product of people actively using violence against others to control their actions or to dominate them in other ways. The literature on abusive spouses, for example, suggests that the violence that develops is not an uncontrolled use of harm but a strategy to manipulate one's partner and control behavior.

It may be only after the fact that the victim comes to see the violence that occurs in relationships as being something other than simply mindless hurting and instead as an instrumental act pressuring him or her to act in a particular way. Victims suffer not only from harmful actions but also from a lack of understanding of "why" the other person acted in this way. So much of the aftermath of these events involves explaining to victims of violence why others would want to use violence against them.

Violence is not always either reactive or proactive. It may be used differently by individuals, depending on how they interpret social situations or on their view of how interaction should take place. As we have suggested, we believe most people have a point at which they themselves would use violence to solve a problem, if only in response to violent acts directed at them. Further, it is evident that otherwise peaceful individuals may escalate conflict to violence simply as they become impatient or frustrated with less dramatic means to deal with these problems. People talk about such inclinations, although, again, rarely do they act out these strategies unless they see that their choices are limited. Still, we have examples of people who act in violent ways who we would not expect to do this. The bank executive who assaulted an airline hostess on a plane may be as incapable of explaining why he did this (not likely the normal way in which he gets service) as the young tough who complained that he was bored prior to popping an unsuspecting victim. Both individuals appeared to run out of options of how to manage others and to get something they wanted (more booze and more excitement, respectively). Violence becomes an option under these circumstances, surprisingly, even in the face of the not unpredictable consequences of severe sanctions for these actions.

What we might say, then, is that violence is one alternative in dealing with others that, in civil society, is not completely removed from other forms of persuasion or coercion. For example, the parent who loses patience with a recalcitrant child and hits him likely would be upset to see the child do the same with a peer. And yet this action has a desired result—to get the child's attention and compliance. Violence, then, is routinized as an option that some people never use but acknowledge as a possibility if pushed. At the same time, it may be a routine that some use all of the time. Its use is determined by many factors, which we will examine in detail in the following chapters.

Outline of the Book

The current study explores conflict in society to determine the social roots of violence. In the next chapter we review the literature on criminal offenders and aggressive acts. We summarize how the literature has focused on offenders and how this has negated an integrated view of violence, particularly through a lack of attention to the role of the victim and in circumstances surrounding aggressive acts. We use the criticisms of theories of crime and aggression to set the stage for an integrated approach to the study of violence and aggression. Chapter 3 provides a detailed summary of the theoretical basis for a theory of routine conflict, drawing upon three different approaches to the study of crime and violence. First, a social constructionist approach is used to define the acceptability of violence in society. Second, the criminal event perspective allows us to explain how crime is a process, including a description of the steps people follow in moving into and out of a violent act. Last, social interactionist theory is used to explain how disputes may be acts of coercion.

Chapter 4 describes the data sources for this study. It outlines the procedures we used in conducting a large-scale survey of conflict and violence in two provinces in Canada. It discusses the methodological assumptions we make about the social roots of violence, and it presents an overview of individuals' experiences with conflict. The chapter seeks to describe the extent of actual conflict in society.

Chapter 5 assesses what social factors may explain the approval of violence and aggression. We present results of our analysis of standardized questions on the societal approval of violence. We present findings from a factorial survey of aggression to demonstrate differences across social groups in their willingness to use aggressive actions in a variety of confrontations. It is in this chapter that we identify the social relationships that we expect to have the greatest impact in creating violent outcomes. These include structural position, gender differences, situational factors, and level of upset. We discuss the mechanisms that people suggest that they would use to manage their social interactions, both in the active application of violence or in avoidance of this violence.

Chapter 6 provides a summary of respondents' accounts of how actual conflicts evolve. We use the criminal event perspective to examine the precursors, transactions, and aftermaths of aggression and violence. We address the role that third parties play in affecting the choices that people make in situations of conflict. We show how third parties may participate in conflict to increase, or decrease, the likelihood of violence. Or, they may act as guardians in situations where they observe, control, document, or punish violent behavior. This chapter also explores the role that coercive actions may play in influencing the directions that people may go in dealing with interpersonal problems.

In chapter 7, Stephen Baron applies our routine conflict theory to a study of street kids to contrast their approval of violence and acts of violence to findings about the general population, as presented in chapters 4 through 6. An analysis of street kids provides important insights into how violence is sanctioned and how it may be considered an important aspect of day-to-day interaction.

Finally, in chapter 8, we summarize the findings of our research, offering some conclusions about what may be done to address interpersonal violence and identifying some unanswered questions. We conclude by addressing some practical issues about violence, particularly in terms of prescribing alternatives to individuals as ways of reducing the use of violence in daily life.

Chapter 2

⊰◈⊱

Learning Aggression and Violence

Introduction

Research on aggression has been dominated by a focus on the reactions of individuals or on the specific acts that aggressive people commit. While this literature is important in that it demonstrates the potential range of the violent response of individuals, it is less helpful in providing predictive statements about who will act in violent ways (beyond suggesting a psychological propensity among those who are easily frustrated to be violent) or in accounting for variations in the context in which violent behavior may occur. In this chapter, we review the literature on aggression starting with the social learning approaches that have been popular over the last two decades. We examine the critiques of these theories, particularly those that have concentrated on the predisposition to act in certain ways as a result of low self-control. From this discussion, we set out the research context in which we offer a theory of routine conflict to be discussed in the next chapter.

Social Learning and Aggression

Social learning theorists have argued that an individual's learning and social experiences, coupled with the individual's thoughts, perceptions, and values, determine behavior (Bandura 1986). Aggression, like other forms of social behavior, is something that people learn through either direct experience or observing the behavior of others. When aggression is rewarded, according to this approach, individuals learn the benefits of repeating the actions of others who are aggressive. In addition, the environment can play a role in limiting opportunities for aggressive behavior.

There has been extensive research in the psychological literature on aggression (see Baron and Richardson 1994). This research, typified by Berkowitz (1989), has focused on the reactive nature of the protagonist in interaction. This work has emphasized the importance of psychological factors, such as frustration, leading to aggressive action over situational factors that appear in violent situations. Zillman (1983, 1988) suggests, however, that to understand the reasons for aggression, we need to know more about the individual than just what is learned. We must take into account, as well, an individual's capacity to control his or her own behavior. For example, high levels of physiological arousal interfere with cognitive processing. Individuals who more easily lose control of their emotions become more vulnerable to environmental cues and impulsivity.

In an attempt to include the role that social forces and cognitive processes play in aggressive behavior, Berkowitz (1988, 1989) has refined his approach by developing the "cognitive–neoassociation" model. This model suggests two things. First, when one is exposed to aversive events (e.g., personal insults), this creates aggressive tendencies to the degree that it arouses negative affect resulting in emotions, thoughts, and memories related to flight (i.e., fear) and fight (i.e., aggression). In the early stages of this process, individuals may respond reactively without any consideration for the motives or emotions of others. They respond in an automatic fashion. This appears to characterize the actions of the "stone killer," an individual who, for no apparent reason, kills. The reaction to the aversive stimulus is considered an involuntary response (although it is hard to conceive of boredom, as in the case of the stone killer, being the likely trigger to a violent response). Nonetheless, this perspective does suggest that frustration can set off violent and aggressive tendencies, with little accommodation made to the circumstances or consequences of the act.

In the later stages of the interaction, however, the impulsive violent reaction may be mediated by taking into consideration the factors that lie behind the provocation. For example, when bumped by a stranger, an individual may react aggressively unless the stranger quickly offers an apology for the action. According to Berkowitz, the apology forces a reevaluation of the action and a reappraisal of the situation. Aggressive behavior is more likely to occur if an individual perceives that the mistreatment is intentional. The interaction that treats the individual unfairly can legitimately provoke aggression. This judgment of fairness echoes the theme of shame or loss of self-esteem that Gilligan pursued in analyzing the violent men he studied. The violence is committed as a way of righting perceived wrongs and saving face.

The cognitive–neoassociation approach to aggression has been criticized for its attempt to overgeneralize the impact of the negative effects of social environments in which individuals operate. As Baron and Richardson (1994) state, Berkowitz contends that aggression stems from negative affect, regardless of its source. "All sources of such affect can hardly be eliminated from the social and physical world. . . . The fact that they cannot be removed, therefore, raises serious doubts concerning the ultimate effectiveness of control strategies based largely upon the removal of such conditions" (p. 311).

Tedeschi and Felson (1994) pursue this criticism further, suggesting that aggression theories are inadequate for explaining the roots of violence because they are based on an incorrect assumption that there is an automatic relationship between aversive stimuli and reactive aggression. The automatic aggressive response to an attack, considered out of the context of the how and why of the situation in which it occurs, ignores the important role that all parties have in defining events as supporting a violent response (p.368). Further, it is not at all clear in social learning theory how aggressive skills can be differentiated from nonaggressive skills in the absence of social contexts.

As Tedeschi and Felson state, social learning theory elucidates the processes through which people develop expectations, values, and conflict styles. The learning history of the individual provides information that allows predictions about individual differences in coercive behavior. "However, the theory is not very informative about the situational factors that elicit coercion" (p. 369). Further, there is no reference to motives associated with justice and identity. In sum, social learning fails to project what people learn about how to manage conflict situations in the context of the situations themselves. Without this elaboration, the ability to determine whether or not behavior will turn violent is greatly diminished.

Low Self-control

Gottfredson and Hirschi (1993) offer a different critique of the aggression theories.[1] They are critical of the assumption that the actor is at the mercy of forces beyond the immediate situation over which she or he has no control (p. 49). Gottfredson and Hirschi claim that their social control model addresses the inadequacies of these approaches through its ability to account for the versatility of offenders where violence and theft are typically found in the same offender. Further, the frustration–aggression model tends to be act specific or behavior specific and, as such, overlooks good evidence for a general tendency in individuals to engage in or avoid criminal acts (Gottfredson and Hirschi 1993).

Gottfredson and Hirschi, in their articulation of a General Theory of

Crime, suggest that criminal behavior is not much different in character than behavior that is noncriminal. Rather, criminal acts contain elements common to all behavior. As a consequence, the general theory does not require that we seek out specific explanations of aggression (e.g., the effects on violence that come from watching violent television programs). Instead, they argue, we need to examine general patterns of individual behavior that are consistent with the tendency toward aggression. For Gottfredson and Hirschi (1990) , the key element in understanding aggression is the fact that people who lack self-control will tend to be impulsive, insensitive, physical (as opposed to mental), risk taking, short sighted, nonverbal, and they will tend therefore to engage in criminal and analogous acts (p. 90). Noncriminal acts may include a wide variety of behaviors such as smoking, drinking, and accidents, and these acts will be engaged in at a relatively high rate by persons with low self-control (p. 91).

Gottfredson and Hirschi (1990) assert that self-control is established in early childhood socialization. Further, they suggest that these traits tend to persist through life, ". . . comprising a stable construct useful in the explanation of crime" (p. 91). Coupled with low self-control is the convenience and opportunity provided to individuals to commit crime. The offender is drawn to the criminal act or an analogous act that is "imprudent," such as smoking, drinking, or gambling, by the immediate gratification it offers (Arneklev et al. 1993). The object of the offense, in Gottfredson's and Hirschi's (1990) terms, is pleasure. "The impulsive or shortsighted person fails to consider the negative or painful consequences of his acts; the insensitive person has fewer negative consequences to consider; the less intelligent person also has fewer negative consequences to consider" (p. 95).

In their analysis of aggression, Gottfredson and Hirschi highlight the importance of considering previous states that create a predisposition to act in a certain way. This is based on socialization. It outlines for individuals the appropriate manner in which they should respond to interaction. Individuals who possess lower levels of self-control will have greater problems with interaction, as their repertoires of action are more limited and they act more impulsively. This theory appears consistent with a view that individuals adopt a routine manner in which they learn to act aggressively or violently. Gottfredson and Hirschi propose that low self-control is simply one consequence of poor socialization, leading to crime. As the level of self-control remains relatively stable throughout life, the routines learned are not likely to be unlearned. The aggressive nature of these individuals will remain constant, controlled only by opportunity and circumstance.

Gottfredson and Hirschi do not dismiss the idea of learning. But, in their view, it is learning in the early years in families and at school that sets the direction for later behavior. The models provided to individuals, as well as their success or failure in controlling their behavior, offer important cues about how punishment works and the likelihood that they will suffer from it when they stray (p. 101). At the same time, Gottfredson and Hirschi complain that most influential theories of crime and delinquency ". . . deny the connection between crime and talking back, yelling, pushing, and shoving, insisting on getting one's way, trouble in school, and poor school performance" (p. 102). This may translate into low self-control that is manifest as a predisposition to act in ways that are aggressive or antisocial.

Akers (1991) criticizes Gottfredson and Hirschi for failing to define self-control separately from the propensity to commit crimes. It seems plausible to incorporate an idea of the propensity that is altered through learning over one's lifetime with a view of self-control that is learned in one's youth. Coupled with low self-control, aggressive repertoires may be learned from others and can have the effect of increasing the chance that crimes will be committed by these individuals. It is not that difficult to see that these learned conflict styles offer a form of motivation to act, based on an assessment of proximate circumstances, including the reactions of others and the likelihood of punishment. In pursuing this point further, Laub and Sampson (1993) suggest that Gottfredson and Hirschi ignore the role of changes in social circumstances that may alter the life trajectories of individuals with low self-control. Gottfredson and Hirschi argue that correlations among adult behaviors (for example, job stability and crime) are completely spurious and should disappear once controls are introduced for prior individual-level differences in criminal propensity or low self-control (p. 305). Laub and Sampson disagree, contending that their research on crime through the life course does not support an assumption of invariance of self-control. They believe that experience in adulthood can have an effect on those who have developed low self-control. Criminality is not simply a function of self-selection by these individuals into risky categories. This suggests, in contradiction to the prediction by Gottfredson and Hirschi, that individuals who exhibit low self-control may learn ways of restricting the damaging consequences of acting on their impulses.

Beyond the criticism of the view that self-control is invariant, Barlow (1991) argues that Gottfredson and Hirschi do not develop the opportunity side of their theory sufficiently well to predict which acts individuals are likely to commit (at a higher or lower rate) at any given time (p. 237). Nor do they offer suggestions for deducing what kind of social or cultural setting would experience a high or low rate of any particular crime or act. Since the criticism by Barlow, there have been some attempts to address these issues through comprehensive tests of the general theory.[2]

Grasmick et al. (1993) provide a detailed test of the general theory as it relates to crime, while Arneklev et al. (1993) examine it as it relates to analogous acts, or what they refer to as imprudent behavior. In both papers, the researchers provide a detailed index of self-control measures that tap the different dimensions of the nominal definitions suggested by Gottfredson and Hirschi. In addition to the self-control measures, Grasmick et al. use measures of opportunity, defined by the ease with which individuals would be able to commit a criminal act.

In their research, Grasmick et al. (1993) report that the interaction of self-control and crime opportunity significantly predicts both fraud and force, based on self-reports from respondents (p. 23). The predictions of the theory are generally supported, they say, but they are left with some concerns. Particularly, they argue that Gottfredson and Hirschi have paid too little attention to the source of variation in opportunity. In a rejoinder, Hirschi and Gottfredson (1993) claim that self-control and opportunity are not independent. While opportunities to commit crime may be limitless, opportunities to commit certain types of crime are restricted by access to certain jobs or certain locations. They say ". . . the generality of the theory thus stems from its conception of the offender, a conception that must be taken into consideration before situational or "structural" influences can be understood" (p. 50).

There is, in this debate as well, the concern that the general theory offers an explanation of crime that is tautological: that is, it explains criminality (low self-control) as a consequence of low self-control. Gottfredson and Hirschi say in their defense that these two factors are different, as the crime is an act predicted by certain characteristics of an actor that include self-control. They say we can resolve the problem of tautology by developing better measures of self-control that parallel but are not the same as the propensity to commit crime. These include smoking, drinking, employment instability, and so on: factors that we could identify as "imprudent" in individuals' lives.

Arneklev et al. (1993) explore the factors that would predict imprudent behavior. They find some support for the theory that shows a relationship between low self-control and drinking and gambling. They report that there is no relationship between self-control and smoking. Arneklev et al. suggest that there is a need to rethink some aspects of the general theory in light of their findings. They propose that an improvement may be made by separating the concept of self-control from risk taking since "[in] such a causal chain, risk seeking is a more proximate determinant of crime and imprudence than is low self-control and, thus, would be expected to have a stronger deterrent effect" (p. 243). This suggests a need to take into account the more proximate factors affecting criminality that may intercede between the direct effect of self-control on these behaviors (see Felson 1994; Miethe and Meier 1994).

We know from previous research on routine activities theory that variations in lifestyle are related to criminal victimization. Felson (1994) makes a strong case for the importance of self-control in how people make assessments about risk taking in their everyday lives. He sees a distinction between staying out of trouble or getting into it, depending on self-control as being compatible with routine activities, in that different activities may provide the opportunity and temptation to act in criminal ways. It is important to address the role that lifestyle has in transmitting and sharing views that promote the expression of hostile feelings in personal interaction by using personal force. Who you are should affect how you approach conflict situations, that is, your propensity toward getting involved in aggressive behavior. This in turn will be modified by who the other persons in a dispute are, as well as by what they do (Luckenbill and Doyle 1989) and by situational factors (Bernard 1990).

General Theory and Routine Conflict

While we agree with Gottfredson's and Hirschi's criticism of act-specific determinants of aggression, we do not accept the deterministic character of the self-control theory that they propose. We can borrow from the general theory the idea that violent outcomes derive from ongoing social interaction and are not a product of some special form of criminal motivation. This routinized nature of violence comes in part from low self-control but, in contradiction to the predictions made by Gottfredson and Hirschi, we argue that low self-control is not invariant and not deterministic in its effects on the range and selection of choices that are made in interaction. Instead, these choices are heavily influenced by the actions of others and by the circumstances under which the interaction takes place.

In a recently published paper, we have tested the relationship between self-control, risky lifestyles, aggressive behavior, and criminal activity (Forde and Kennedy 1997). The analyses presented there shows that elements of low self-control do not directly affect criminal behavior, although measures of self-control have strong effects on imprudent behavior that relate, in turn, to offending. Explanations of criminality are mediated by opportunity variables that relate to the exposure to crime that comes with certain lifestyles and the extent to which individuals suggest that they would act aggressively in confrontational situations. Not unlike the criticism of aggression theories that say that individuals simply react violently from frustration, by saying that people with low self-control will be violent is highly circumscribed and not very elucidating. Further, it lacks precision. There are too many people who have low self-control that are not violent. Given that we find that proximate conditions intervene between self-control and arrest, for example, is it not possible to change proximate conditions so that they work to reduce the likelihood of crime outcomes? These changes can include changing opportunities for risky lifestyles, enhancing anger management skills, and so on.

While our research shows that self-control has an effect on crime behavior, we are less than impressed by the use of this variable as a key factor in explaining variations in individual aggressiveness and violence. This is partly because of the difficulty encountered in operationalizing this measure, as Gottfredson and Hirschi would have us do, looking at the ways in which people fix their propensity to act in certain ways in early childhood and assuming that this stays invariant over their lifetime. Also, our results show that opportunity is necessary for self-control to have any effect on criminal behavior. Further, knowing that people with low self-control are more likely to misbehave tells us less than knowing the conditions under which these behaviors appear. The general theory holds up in its effort to identify the *latent traits* (Gottfredson and Hirschi 1993) one can use to identify who is more likely to be crime prone. However this proneness is not a criminal tendency per se but is highly contextualized, based on past experience, lifestyle, and learning. Our respecification sees the general theory of crime conforming nicely to the new approaches in criminology that suggest a more integrated (and global) approach to the study of crime occurrence, focusing less on motivation and more on the total crime event (see Miethe and Meier 1994; Sacco and Kennedy 1996).

Taking these criticisms into account, we will structure the analysis of violence and aggression that focuses on self-control to examine the choices that people make under different circumstances. A restriction in choices may be a function of low self-control or it may not. The answer to this is not really that important for our purpose (although our research shows that in adults, at least, there seems to be a connection). What we believe more important in analyzing the social roots of violence are the ways in which individuals construct their social environment and how they conduct themselves based on their concerns about the actions of others.

Summary

This chapter has described some of the details of how social learning and self-control theories approach the study of aggression and violence. We discuss the major assumptions of each theory and examine some problems for each in how they explain the origin of violence in society. We argue that both types of theories have made important contributions to the literature on aggression and crime, but that a theory that considers how individuals exercise choices depending on circumstances and past experience will provide a better explanation of violent behavior.

Social learning theories have made strong contributions to our understanding of how offenders come to learn to be aggressive and to use violence. We find, however, that the literature on social learning is unable to account for the versatility of offenders across different situations and for the importance of situational factors that may explain how some people may better manage or others may intervene in conflict situations.

Self-control also is an important aspect of learning and has a role to play in affecting the level of aggressiveness that individuals display in social interaction. A weakness of self-control theory, as presented by Gottfredson and Hirchi, is that self-control need not be seen as invariant. The assumption that individuals set up their repertoires of action early in life and are unable to change these over time has been shown to be unfounded (see Sampson and Laub 1993). Further, self-control effects are mediated by the opportunities provided by the environment (Forde and Kennedy 1997).

In the next chapter, we will focus on the role that social context can play in setting up violence. We will consider the importance of social construction, coercion, and the dynamics of the event in assessing the structure, content, and process involved in aggressive action. We will then offer an outline of a theory of routine conflict that will provide the framework for our data analysis later in the book.

Chapter 3

Elements of Routine Conflict: Social Construction, Coercion, and the Social Event

Introduction

Theoretical approaches to violent criminal offenders have been heavily weighted to a study of the offender, searching for his or her motivation in the breakdown of social control (Hirschi 1969); on social disorganization (Bursik and Grasmick 1993; Shaw and McKay 1942); or peer pressure to defy authority (Agnew 1992). More recently, victims have become an important focus of crime analysis, but like studies on motivated offenders, this research has considered victims exclusive of the situational contexts in which they operate (Hindelang, Gottfredson, and Garofalo 1978). As we pointed out in chapter 1, recent theoretical efforts have sought to provide a more integrated approach to crime occurrence in which we find situational factors taking on more prominence in criminological explanation, where offenders, victims, and circumstances of their interaction are all considered simultaneously (Birkbeck and LaFree 1993; Miethe and Meier 1994; Sacco and Kennedy 1996).

We have said that we need to account for three different aspects of violence to fully understand its origins through an integrated perspective. These include, first of all, the social construction of violence, based on definitions (legal and otherwise), values, accepted practice, and situation, all of which may influence how people characterize the acceptability, harm, and appropriate reaction for responding to violent acts. Second, we believe we can better understand violence as part of a process, characterized as an event in which there are definable stages prior to violence and in the aftermath of a social transaction. Borrowing from the criminal event perspective (Sacco and

Kennedy 1996), we can account for this process and apply it to an analysis of interpersonal conflict. Third, we believe violence can be best understood in terms of its instrumental character, particularly relating to the use of violence to coerce others to act in compliance with the demands of an aggressor. This view of violence projects it beyond a simple and automatic response to anger and frustration. Violence becomes an important vehicle for obtaining certain specified outcomes within interaction. We have combined the elements of construction, process, and content into a theory of routine conflict that suggests that individuals come into interactions with certain expectations that are formed by previous experiences, socialization, and the behavior of others. These expectations help determine whether or not individuals will see violence as an option in dealing with conflict or aggressive behavior. While this theory is grounded on a complex array of factors, its basic assumption is that choices are made based on the constraints of situations and the repertoires learned by the protagonists in these and similar encounters. In this chapter we will examine the component parts of this theory before showing how it can be used in the study of violence.

The Social Construction of Violence

There is public consensus over the need to combat violent crime in modern society (Reiss and Roth 1993). However, there is a basic problem in establishing what is acceptable and what is not in the use of force and aggression, even when this behavior involves what objectively can be defined as harm to the victim. This idea has been explored in the literature on the criminogenic nature of mainstream culture, where cultural representations—in popular culture, the media, public discussions of social behavior, and the socialization of children (Sykes and Matza 1957)—portray violence as being an acceptable means of dealing with problems. Given the prevalence of violence as a mainstream value in society, we believe it is important to start any analysis of violence with the statement that (with some exceptions of serious forms of crimes, such as murder and sexual assault) not everyone will agree that violence constitutes, in all cases, inappropriate behavior.

There are cultural phenomenon that socially legitimate the use of violence (Straus 1985). In the United States, Straus has found that factors such as the preference for violent television programs, participation in socially approved violent activities, including college football, and the use of corporal punishment in schools exhibit regional differences, with higher levels in the West and South. These high levels of legitimate violence are correlated with high levels of homicide. The acceptable levels of crime, then, may actually vary regionally, depending on the values people place on the legitimate use of physical force. Public support for violence may be complemented by public support for enforcement or capital punishment.

Crime of some sort is evident in all societies. This has led some scholars to argue that crime itself is an inevitable part of the development of social control (Durkheim 1964). Does this mean that violence too is an inevitable consequence of social interaction? To talk about the inevitability of violence does not promote the view that it is unavoidable. It does suggest, though, that violence often is seen as an alternative to more peaceful problem solving, even among individuals who have rarely, if ever, used this option. We are confronted in our society with depictions in the news media and in popular culture (films, video, television) of individuals who defend themselves against attackers using violence, and we see their action as positively extolled. For example, the avenger, as portrayed by Clint Eastwood, is glorified when he dispatches the villains with lethal violence. The bad guys deserved their fate, we reason, through their overt use of force and by their attacks on innocent victims. This situational justification of the use of violence is played out again and again in cases where the victim (or victim's advocate) uses violence as a way of seeking justice. The social construction of this event in this way characterizes this violence as being publicly acceptable, even honorable.

There are many modern-day examples of this justification. Allowing individuals to arm themselves—many states have passed laws that allow people to carry concealed weapons—promotes the view that there are situations in which the use of guns against others is acceptable. Louisiana has just passed a law where deadly force may be justified as a defense against a potential carjacker (someone who threatens you while you are in your car). The right to have and use guns is promoted by researchers such as Gary Kleck (1996) in arguments that banning weapons will increase the vulnerability of people who need them for self-defense and will lead to an increase of criminal victimization. While Kleck assumes that these individuals will use weapons only as a last resort and only when they are threatened by others wielding arms, there is a point at which gun use is legitimated.

A recent case in California makes us wonder if the justification of violence used in self-defense is always clear-cut. In early 1994, a young man approached two teenagers underneath an underpass in Los Angeles. The teenagers were involved in painting graffiti on the walls. What happened next seems to be in question, but it would appear that the young man confronted them (he says he feared robbery by the kids, who threatened him with screwdrivers). What is indisputable is that one of the teenagers died, shot in the back by the young man. The other teen ended up in the hospital with gun wounds.

The reaction to this crime included people extolling the young man's actions in attacking the teens. People who claim to be tired of the social disorder of inner-city neighborhoods hailed the young man as being a hero for his actions. The man himself did not shy away from the publicity. In fact, he claimed that the victim's mother should be held responsible for the death. Had she raised him properly, the victim would not have been defacing others' property. The victim brought this retribution on himself and so did his mother, through neglect. This tragic story is made even more tragic by the deep level of support afforded a young man, seemingly provoked only by a spray can, who felt compelled to seek his own form of street justice. Capital punishment for vandalism seems severe, yet the rules of the street appear to permit and even condone it.

This case should be considered in light of the aftermath of the Bernard Goetz killings. While Goetz initially was widely acclaimed for his shooting of his "attackers" on a New York City subway train, public support waned when a number of details about the case were revealed. It was discovered that Goetz had armed himself and then went on the subway in search of trouble to seek revenge for an earlier mugging he had suffered. In addition, in the confrontation with the youths he subsequently shot, it was not clear that they were robbing him. Rather, it appears they asked him for change. Goetz shot one of the individuals in the back as he was fleeing the scene and posed no further danger to him. Goetz was acquitted of all charges laid against him, including attempted murder and assault, but he was found guilty of illegal possession of a handgun (Adler et al. 1991).[1]

There are a number of specific factors that can influence how people judge violent acts. Of great importance is what individual bystanders view as the relationship between the combatants in a personal dispute. Shotland and Straw (1976) argue that bystanders are less likely to intervene in a violent assault perpetrated by a man against a woman if they perceive them to be married rather than strangers. Also, Davis (1991) points out that when people witness adults physically abusing children in public, they show reluctance to intervene in a "private matter." While these examples do not necessarily suggest that bystanders condone the violence they witness, they ignore it or fail to stop it partly because they feel it is none of their business. Implicitly, they see the violent action as being a part of the acceptable, if still repugnant, interaction that takes place between intimates. The standard defense of individuals who fail to intervene in family abuse situations has been that if they did, not only the abuser but also the victim would turn on them. Again, this story suggests that there is compliance by both parties in the abusive relationship that somehow requires that others tolerate this violence.

Further elements in our definition of social situations that excuse violent interaction include the need to not be mocked or humiliated, or the need to control others in intimate relations (as suggested by the excuse that the physical punishment of children is acceptable because they pay attention to their parents more readily when they are spanked than when they are verbally chastised). It is, in sum, by no means the case that our society universally abhors violence. There are many situations in which it is permitted, condoned, and even encouraged.

Defining what is normative behavior is confounded by our reactions to actions that accompany changes in morality. Gibbs (1981) asks with what frequency must a type of act occur before it is considered a norm (p. 14)? Further, what percentage of agreement do we need in the population to guarantee that the public would see certain behavior as being acceptable (p. 11)? Similarly, Currie (1985) asks what level of punishment is necessary to guarantee that we have reached an optimal level of social order? What level of enforcement of laws ensures that we have safe streets and homes? This assumes that there is some common standard that we use to judge safety. In fact, levels of safety and security are relative to other parts of the city or to other times when safety was higher or lower. Are we safer now that crime rates have begun to go down, or do we simply feel more secure because we appear to be handling the crime problem? So much of how we view these problems is a function of our tolerance for general threat and our assessment of personal risk.

This judgment of risk is used not only by the public but also is applied differentially by law enforcement agencies in their control of violent and aggressive behavior. The designation of violence as being criminal may be influenced by important considerations that will affect how the law is applied, as a strong reaction to violent action. It is not enough then to simply say that someone has been hit (that a violent act has occurred) to conclude that this act is harmful and needs sanction (Black 1992; Felson and Steadman 1983). We must know not only what these definitions entail but also how definitions of violence are developed. Further, the negotiation of justice may be a reflection not only of what the agents of social control can do, but it also reflects what they are prepared to do in attacking violence (Kennedy 1990).

As an example of this, we see contradictions developing in police agencies that are empowered to deal with violent crime that impose situational criteria in deciding how to handle cases of interpersonal violence. There has been a tremendous concern about the growth of violence in schools. Whereas before, school officials would break up fights and deal with the culprits through internal school sanctions, the current practice has school authorities calling the police to break up these altercations. What previously would be treated as a fight is now treated as a case of violent crime (an assault).

At the same time, police agencies that are confronted with overwhelming demand create decision rules about how to deal with calls they receive through their emergency phone lines. One way of prioritizing these calls involves a screening technique that puts lower emphasis on certain types of events. An assault between two males where there is no need for immediate action (e.g., the harm is not serious and the offender is not present) elicits quite a different response than does a domestic conflict. By not dispatching a car to deal with this type of problem and encouraging the reporting of this to a ministation, as is the practice in one city, the police suggest that one situation requires a different response than the other. While they will act on a complaint, their action (or inaction) reflects the public's mood about differential allocation of scarce police resources in dealing with violence. We need the police to deal with the "serious" problems (school violence and domestic disputes) and to let the other "less serious" cases (conflict between two males) resolve themselves with minimal police involvement. These decision rules clearly mirror a social construction of the threat to social order and the harm done in these cases. It is clear that some behavior not dealt with through the formal application of law may be disorderly, threatening, or dangerous. For example, bar fights are strictly illegal and yet there often are no arrests, even when the police intervene. Police may leave the handling of altercations in taverns to bouncers. As long as there has not been a major injury, the main desired outcome of these encounters is a return to order.

Informal responses are not without consequence for the offender. These can include the victim fighting back, enlisting the help of others to gain retribution, denying the offender future access to interaction, or shunning the offender. These strategies comprise what Black (1992) has called "self-help." Self-help develops when police or formal agencies will or can do nothing to deal with the violence. "Rough justice" may be used when the "victims" do not wish to deal with the police and will strike out against the "offender" (Kennedy 1988; Skogan 1984). People may perceive that the only way to handle a problem is through personal action. This also may work to legitimize violence.

Self-help often appears to be premeditated. It is for this reason that women who kill their husbands after years of abuse have been convicted of murder. As we pointed out earlier, in the past courts have decided that unless the woman has an immediate threat to her life (that is, she is acting in self-defense), the violent action is not defensible in this way. However, accounts of these events have shown that, in many instances, these women feel that they can no longer protect themselves and their children. They believe, further, that no one else can either. For this reason, some observers have argued that this violence is actually acceptable. While the courts have resisted excusing the violence of killing per se, they have allowed the introduction of evidence of battering as an acceptable defense in these situations.

Violence as an Event

The actual experience with violence is contained in a complex array of situational and contextual factors that directly affect the nature of the interaction, or criminal event, and its outcome. Routine activities theory suggests that it is the lifestyles of victims that make them vulnerable to victimization. Opportunity for crime comes in the convergence in space and time of motivated offenders and vulnerable victims in the absence of capable guardians (Cohen and Felson 1979). A second approach, rational choice theory, focuses on the situational choices of potential offenders (Clarke 1992). From these two perspectives, the decision to offend depends on the opportunity to commit a crime. This involves a judgment of whether or not the offender will get away with the offense, including using violence as a coercive device. Opportunity, however, is an emergent concept that is not predetermined. It is defined through the interaction of the lifestyles of potential victims, offenders, and other parties. In recent years, as a consequence of changes in daily living routines, there are more ways in which offenders and victims converge in time and space. Opportunities are now afforded for the commission of crime, whereas in past history, with different lifestyles, these opportunities were more limited. For example, a greater proportion of women entering the labor force provides more targets for victimization outside of the home and more opportunities for the burglarizing of empty houses.

A sizable amount of research has indicated that the basic premise of routine activities theory is supportable, that is, that changing lifestyles have created routine activities that have increased opportunities for crime (Cohen and Felson 1979; Kennedy and Forde 1990a). These risky lifestyles are found in groups that represent particularly high concentrations of both victims and offenders. In this analysis, it is the outcome of these lifestyles (high offending and high victimization) that confirms the efficacy of this theoretical perspective (Kennedy and Forde 1990b).

Routine activities theory focuses the risk of victimization around the varying levels of opportunity. Rational choice theory explains how opportunity is maximized. Rational choice theorists propose that criminal behavior takes on the character of an economic decision, where judgments are made about the costs and benefits of committing crime. According to Cornish (1993), this decision is based on situational factors that contribute to an offender's assessment of the suitability of targets and the selection of crime commission methods. The rational choice perspective advocates, in response to these decisions, situational crime prevention methods that raise the cost of crime commission to the degree that offenders are deterred and, therefore, do not choose to act criminally.

In discussing these choices, Cornish suggests that there is a need to understand more about connections between crime and particular sorts of lifestyles. The factors that coincide with crime occurrence lead us to pay attention to the dynamics of the interaction, as much as to the reasons the offender may have for committing the crime in the first place. Rational choice theory downplays the suggestion, from subcultural theory, that individual action may be explained as a function of values that are brought to the situation. More important than values are the calculations people make about how the situation will benefit them. The constraints of the group may be part of this calculation (loss of social support, for example), but this would seem to be more of an external factor to be judged in terms of costs, as opposed to an internal value that controls behavioral choice.

Rational choice theory makes much of the need to account for the present orientation of individuals involved in interaction. In doing this, Cornish (1993) admits, it might seem to pay less attention to the longer-term chains of learning by which individuals develop motivation and abilities (or freedom from constraints) in order to commit crimes (p. 366). However, this focus, Cornish argues, simply changes the premium placed on accounting for the early life history of individuals or the characteristics that motivate people to crime (see also Sampson and Laub 1993). Instead, the proximate factors to the crime event are made more important in the assessment of outcomes. The event provides the cues for behavior rather than behavior, per se, predetermining the outcome of the event. For example, in a life course-approach, we might assume that people age out of criminality as a result of a change in their tendencies to commit crime, while an event-based approach would argue that people stop committing crime because as they age the costs become more prohibitive and greatly outweigh the benefits.

In arguing the case of rational choice theory, Cornish provides a pragmatic view of crime as an outcome of the convergence of offenders with opportunities that will reward them if it can be obtained at low cost. The obvious choice in these situations is to assault or kill. The solution to prevent these outcomes is to remove the opportunity or increase the cost of acquisition. These decisions are made in the present and reflect an ongoing set of calculations that work to benefit the offender or to deter him or her.

In developing applications of these theories, the situational factors that contribute to criminal outcomes are increasingly being viewed as interconnected. The social structural factors that connect to crime (Meier and Miethe 1993) and the precursors and aftermath of criminal events (Sacco and Kennedy 1996) suggest that there is a social dynamic that occurs in the crime process that transcends the simple act of committing a crime. Context can provide an important controller on the ways in which decisions are made by individuals in the interaction prior to and after the offense occurs.

In looking at crime as events, we can see elements of both routine activities and rational choice theories playing a part. But while these explanations seem to provide a strong basis upon which to explain property crime, they have been poorly developed in the effort to explain the nature of aggressiveness and violence. It does not seem adequate to analyze most violent crime as being a consequence of simple opportunity or as a result of a rational choice that someone makes to benefit from this action (although this may be the case in robbery, it seems less likely the case in assault). While we know that living certain risky lifestyles makes individuals more likely to be victims of violent crime (Kennedy and Forde 1990b), we know little about this outcome other than the fact that the risk is there. There is something missing in this equation that accounts for why these violent acts occur.

The concept of the criminal event (Miethe and Meier 1994; Sacco and Kennedy 1996) proposes an integrated approach to the study of crime based on the view that these events cannot be separated from the physical and social settings in which they occur. In short, the concept of the criminal event encourages us to conceptualize crime in terms that encompass but also extend beyond the study of offenders or victims by themselves. Rather than being individual events, crimes are social events (Sacco and Kennedy 1996). This view of crime accounts for the actions of offenders, victims, and bystanders, all at once. Further, looking at crime as a criminal event allows us to recognize that crime events have a systematic character, in that they are made more or less likely by the choices people make about how and where they spend their time, energy, and money. These events are episodic, having a beginning and an end. In fact, the episodic nature of these events allows us to examine them in terms of the factors that bring about the onset of these acts (the precursors), the transactions themselves, and their aftermath (Sacco and Kennedy 1996). These three stages of the event have distinct qualities that influence the ways in which the act evolves and the actions of various individuals caught up in this event.

The violent act can be understood in terms of cultural factors (including the legitimization of violence), as precursors which suggest ways in which individuals can or cannot act in dealing with others. Legal structures develop to help define the appropriate choices to the settlement of disputes or the coercion of others. These definitions may be mitigated by the nature of the relationship that exists between victims and offenders, the actions of the victims, and the intervention of third parties. The latter may act to accelerate the action to violence, or they may act as intervenors who stop the violence before it occurs.

Of importance in the transaction stage are the interpretations made by the different parties about the actions that take place. The violence itself may be part of an encounter where both parties harm one another, or it may be perpetrated solely by one person on the other. The transaction may be the result of individuals feeling like they are out of options in dealing with others, seeing violence as the only alternative to get the other party to do what they want. It is at this stage as well that the victim may avoid the violence by simply running away or using some other means to deescalate the conflict. Coercion, which we will discuss in the next section, may also play a part in influencing the outcome of transactions.

In the aftermath, a number of factors come into play. There is a judgment made of harm done. There also is an assessment of blame and guilt, possibly leading to a call for punishment to deter future violent acts. Consideration is given to what steps can be taken more generally to stop individuals from acting violently, giving rise to the pressure to change the laws, change police practice, or offer more protection for victims. The decisions made in the aftermath of violence can have important consequences for the ways in which new violent acts come to be seen as options, particularly if potential offenders understand that things have changed in terms of the punishment they are likely to get for being violent.

The criminal event not only accounts for the actions of all parties and the stages that the event goes through, but also takes into account the fact that violence may occur very differently under various types of circumstances. The criminal event perspective provides a time and space framework, with goal setting achieved through the definition of means of getting others to comply with one's wishes. Sacco and Kennedy (1996) have suggested that we can study events through the use of domains, where we acknowledge that very dissimilar types of behavior can occur (and will be defined differently) depending upon whether or not it happens within the family and household, during leisure, or when working. We interact with family members in a way that we do not interact with coworkers. In addition, there has been an opposing view about what is acceptable in the privacy of the home versus what can occur in public. While these views are changing, we still see that family violence has quite separate origins and explanations than violent actions pursued in leisure settings or at work. We want to explore these domain differences in some detail in the following study.

Coercion

A coercive action is taken with the intent of imposing harm on another person or forcing compliance (Tedeschi and Felson 1994). This comes in three forms: threats, bodily force, and punishment. First, threats communicate an intent to do harm. These are uttered in all sorts of contexts, but suggest that the individual is willing to force others to comply through a declaration of intent to harm. The law acknowledges the importance of threat in creating fear. An assault need not involve actual physical contact, as threatening gestures also are included in this category. Second, bodily force is the use of physical contact to compel or constrain the behavior of another person. This also can involve using force to respond to aggression. The harm done through the use of force may be judged by who started the event, the differential size of opponents, and who is to blame for causing the greatest injury.

Finally, punishment is an act intended to do harm. This involves responding to situations where people seek retribution for a slight or for some other injustice. In fact, Jack Katz, in his book *Seductions of Crime* (1988), illustrates how trivial acts may escalate to extreme acts in his analysis of how murderers may consider homicide an act of "righteous slaughter." In these instances, impassioned killers may uphold the social status of husband, mother, wife, or virile male. Despite what may appear to outsiders as being crimes of passion, with no rational motive, Katz describes how many offenders may characterize these events (e.g., shooting an unfaithful husband or wife) as a defense of the morality of the social system and as a personal claim of moral worth (p. 19).

Coercive actions portray the individual as attempting to gain compliance from another rather than looking at the act as simply a reactive form of aggression (which may be both involuntary and unintentional). The actor who uses coercion does so to achieve some end. The way this is done may vary according to the goals that are to be achieved. These include: (1) control of the behavior of others (e.g., sanctioning people who hit their kids); (2) restoring justice (responding to the unfair demands of customers or invalid claims, such as the request to move from one's seat in a stadium); and (3) asserting and protecting identities (such as responding to identity attacks).

In the decision-making process, a series of choices are made about when to use coercion or some other action. As Tedeschi and Felson (1994) say, the basic elements of these decisions include assessing the value of the outcome; making a judgment about the success in achieving that outcome; setting expectations about incurring costs; and minimizing the negative values of costs (p. 350). Decision making may be seen as stages in conflict, where certain preconceptions are brought into the conflict, governing the choices people will make about how to handle these problems. Tedeschi and Felson suggest that coercion, rather than persuasion and inducement, is more likely to be used to achieve compliance in situations of social conflict. Particularly as personal interests diverge, noncoercive approaches are seen as being ineffective. "Escalation may occur when each antagonist meets resistance from the other and when the motives to defend social identities and mete out justice are salient. Levels of harm may be inflicted that outweigh any tangible benefits that could be expected by either person" (p. 352).

The social interactionist perspective of Tedeschi and Felson predicts strong audience effects on the use of coercion. The protection of self-images or social identities that people have may encourage individuals to use aggression or violence to promote a strong personal image that will not be violated through insults. In general, Tedeschi and Felson suggest that the presence of an audience increases identity concerns and the likelihood of retaliation (p.354). What may appear as an unrealistic conflict, then, may actually be firmly embedded in a realistic assessment by protagonists of the need to act forcefully to "save face" or promote a strong and macho self-image.

Specifying a Theory of Routine Conflict

The theory of routine conflict incorporates elements of the perspectives offered by social construction approaches, the criminal event, and social coercion theory. The theory explains that individuals come to situations with a predisposition to act in particular ways—not necessarily in a generically violent fashion. Individuals learn repertoires that they use to manage their daily lives, much as they learn basic aspects of how to live certain lifestyles. These repertoires are socially constructed and govern the ways that they act, providing guidelines that they follow as they progress through different stages of interaction. These guidelines set out the bases for the development of routine conflicts (much as routines develop in daily activities). Also, crime does not stop just because the costs go up as people age, but more importantly, people who commit crimes desist from this because they learn about its consequences and develop ways of avoiding situations that they know will lead to criminal outcomes. Or, people learn to gain compliance from others through noncoercive means and the avoidance of punishment.

The guidelines people use to cue their social interaction are often present oriented, heavily influenced by current situations. However, they are also (as are choices that people make) the function of the ways people have learned to deal with others through witnessing their conflict resolution practices, personal experience, and imagining how one would deal with certain situations. These routines are not numerous. They are guided by general principles of decorum and role playing.

Further, these routines depend on the ways in which people define social situations in activating social behavior. Routines fit into interaction through the playing out of prescribed roles. Choices made are contingent on factors that serve as precursors to violent acts and considerations that are made about the aftermath of these actions, for example, punishments that may serve to deter individuals from acting in this way in future encounters.

Unlike rational choice theory where the assumption is that individuals can make decisions that directly influence the crime outcome, the routine conflict theory works on the assumption that people make incremental choices in their interactions with others, choices that may lead to positive results (e.g., no violence) or to decisions that lead to negative outcomes (e.g., violence). An important factor affecting a decision is the relationship of the other person to the individual.

The key elements in the verification of the theory relate to the factors that influence the evolution of conflict. These include the following: the definition of the situation; the level of individual self-control; the nature of the interaction (for example, the judgment that is made concerning whether or not coercion is an appropriate strategy in controlling the situation); the relationship of the individuals in the interaction; the lifestyles that create sustained exposure to certain types of "risky" situations; the stated procedures that would be used to react to certain situations in certain ways; the social domain in which the interaction takes place; and the means by which interactions are influenced by third parties. Important as well is the emotional element that relates to the level of upset or anger that people feel about the ways in which the conflict evolves.

This approach does not necessitate the assumption that individuals arrive in situations that become violent with malice or with psychopathological tendencies, although clearly those who have these motivations would appear more likely to follow routine conflict strategies that are harmful to others. Others also have the opportunity to avoid or deflect these harmful effects if they understand the nature of the actions and work to neutralize them.

The routine conflict approach borrows from the characterizations by Erving Goffman (1959) of the ways individuals learn how to act through situated transactions. In these transactions, the meaning in the situation is drawn from the ways in which others act toward you. Goffman (1959) viewed situated transactions as processes of interaction involving two or more individuals that last as long as the participants find themselves in the presence of one another. This focus on transaction promotes the idea that we must study what goes on between the participants rather than what any one of them does. From sustained interaction with others, individuals are able to use set repertoires of actions to move through a number of transactions in their daily lives. These repertoires, or styles of behaving, predispose what people do in given situations.

Goffman depicted this interaction as being comparable to being on stage, playing a particular role. This analogy seems appropriate except that we feel more can be gained by looking at individuals operating as moving through frames of a movie. As opposed to being in a play, actors play out roles where the endings are not predetermined but the rules of order are clearly defined. Using this analogy, we can see individuals bringing to situations a set of expectations that influence their behavior at different stages in the interaction. These expectations are formed from previous interactions. It is the iterative aspect of this interaction that provides the important cues to individuals in developing a repertoire of routine conflicts.

These routine cues have been called "scripts." Barley (1986) refers to scripts as outlines of recurrent patterns of interaction that define, in observable and behavioral terms, the essence of the role individuals play as actors in interaction. As they are manifested in the flow of behavior, scripts constitute the standard plots of types of encounters whose repetition defines the settings "interaction order." Barley goes on to suggest that actors' identities are replaced by the positions they play. Their behaviors and speech are reduced to a generic form and content, and the action's evolution can be defined as a series of typical acts. "[S]cripts can therefore be viewed as behavioral grammars that inform a setting's everyday action" (Barley 1986: 83).

Van Brunschot (1996), in a study of assaultive behavior, reports that there are generic patterns of behavior that appear in these cases with domain specific effects influencing assault outcomes. Past experience with assault is an important predictor of the extent to which individuals will be involved in more serious assault events and repeat victimization. Van Brunschot suggests that learned repertoires are important in explaining how individuals find their way back into situations of violence with others.

Similarly, Luckenbill (1977) suggests that murders that occur in informal settings are more likely to involve people who were known to one another. Recent studies using large and representative samples of homicides replicate this finding between victim and offender relationship and its ties with the location of a homicide (e.g., see Silverman and Kennedy 1993). Luckenbill has proposed that these homicides occur as a result of the interaction between the parties involved, rather than as a direct outcome of the behavior of any of the participants considered individually. He suggests that transactions can be understood as if they are "character contests" where efforts on the part of the disputants to "save face" result in deadly combat.

In testing Luckenbill's approach, Savitz, Kumar, and Zahn (1991) report that over half of killings contain an informal contest of character or moral strength, and ". . . although one or both of the parties could have resolved the conflict before it took its final fatal form, they failed to do so" (p. 28). This implies that there is some aspect of interaction in these homicides that promotes a violent outcome, where the fatal outcome seems an inevitable product of the interaction. Half of the cases Savitz, Kumar, and Zahn looked at occurred under circumstances in which the person who was killed precipitated the initial personal offense. The homicide transaction, based on these findings, is clearly dynamic, with no set "offender" or "victim," but rather an outcome that evolves from a set of routine interpersonal dealings that turn violent, and ultimately, deadly.

Cheatwood (1996) reports similar findings to Luckenbill in his research of single-offender homicides in Baltimore. When he looked at multiple-offender murders, however, he found that felony homicides are often unplanned and are the consequence of burglaries or robberies gone bad. While murder might be considered a consequence of their activity, the participants obviously do not consider it that likely, and they are less likely to anticipate it as an outcome. In nonfelony homicide, Cheatwood found that the death of the victim was anticipated prior to entry into the interaction. Each homicide was the culmination of a relationship that covered two or more interactions separated by a few minutes to a few days. Consistent with our assumptions, Cheatwood says that these nonfelony multiple-offender homicides regularly involved a rehearsal for the violence, with the decision to kill happening outside of the final interaction between the victim and the offender. What he concludes is that this research makes it obvious that we must extend the homicide event further into the past and the future than has been our tendency. Cheatwood concludes that we must understand more fully how individuals anticipate "violence" (p. 127).

A final example is provided by Anderson (1994), who identifies the specific criteria used to determine violent behavior among street youth. He suggests that there is regularity in the response to "dissing," whereby individuals determine that certain actions and circumstances have culminated in their being degraded in some way. This is reminiscent of Gilligan's focus on the violent offender's preoccupation with respect. A violent response is judged as an entirely appropriate way to react when one's self-esteem is on the line, suggesting that street youth conform to specific expectations about how one should be treated honorably and consistent with their status. This "code of the street" is identified in other ethnographic studies as well (see Kornhauser 1978).

These examples support the view that there are specific cues and repertoires individuals learn to follow that can be instrumental in leading them to violence. Our study, described in the pages that follow, will investigate these in greater detail, looking at the ways in which the general population describes violence and their experience with the use of violence in social interaction with others.

Summary

This chapter has presented the major propositions of social constructionist, event based, and interactionist theories of crime. From these theories we draw components to include in a routine conflict theory of violence. Among the common elements, we suggest that violence as a situated transaction (which can include a number of interactions that contribute to the construction of a violent event, as suggested by Cheatwood) constitutes the unit of analysis in determining crime outcomes. Included in these transactions are:

(1) the assumption that certain behavior is acceptable and will lead to predictable results; (2) transactions evolve over the time that they take place and different meanings can emerge from them; and (3) people sometimes use or are confronted with coercive behavior. Most crime of this type does not result from the predatory actions of one person toward another. It emerges from conversation, argument, dispute, anger, and confrontation. As interactants switch into these states, the controllers of routine conflict dictate responses that accelerate or reduce the conflict. Part of this sequence is an anticipation on the part of the parties involved of the likely consequences of their actions.

It seems naive to assume that people involved in violence (both as offenders and victims) have not anticipated this as a consequence of their actions. Under what conditions do these aggressive scenarios get played out? Who and what stimulates their emergence? What is likely to stop them from occurring or, if started, to not lead to serious injury? These questions imply that we can anticipate that certain actions in certain situations will lead to violent outcomes, that there is a way of articulating the context of violent repertoires. Yet criminologists seem to avoid the obvious when they analyze these events by looking only at the motivation of the offender who entered into these interactions, bent on injuring the other party.

The emphasis in the rest of the book will be on the dynamic nature of social interaction as it may produce violent responses. The importance of situational factors in helping shape social interaction is added to a perspective that suggests that violence is often used in an instrumental way. Hurting others clearly involves more than an act that occurs from a simple reactive state. Violence is used to get others to do things, to reestablish social relations, or to seek retribution. The interpretation of these "constructions" of violence is important in our understanding of how it evolves and changes. We will weave these themes of construction, coercion, and event through an analysis of people's attitudes and actions in their daily lives. The next chapter presents our study and elaborates on the measures we will use in our test of the theory of routine conflict.

Chapter 4

Studying Routine Conflict and Violence

Introduction

Traditional sources of information about crime (including Uniform Crime Reports and victim surveys) provide much information about incidence and prevalence but very limited information about the etiology of interpersonal conflict. In choosing a research method to test the routine conflict model, we must reflect on our assumptions about interpersonal relations in society. We argue that conflict is a part of everyday life (Forde and Kennedy 1997; Kennedy 1990). Thus we would expect to see forms of conflict in all domains of social interaction. Nonetheless, we also expect that there will be a gradient of conflict where the severe forms of it, such as an aggravated assault, will be far less common.

We decided that a survey research project would provide the best way of collecting primary data about conflict in the community. Of the alternative methods, first, an experimental approach would most likely be too artificial. It also would be unethical to expose persons in a laboratory to high-intensity conflicts, such as an assault, to study their reactions to them. Second, a field study would not allow us to talk to a large number of people about conflict in a wide variety of settings. Third, use of police records would be inadequate, because official statistics are generally recorded as grouped data. More important, they do not record much, if any, information about circumstances that led up to a conflict (although it is possible, as Van Brunschot (1996) has done, to review the police reports to gain more information about what occurred in violent crimes). A further limitation of police records is that these reports provide information only about violence known to the police and judged serious enough by citizens and police to be treated as a crime.

A survey allows us to reach out to a large number of people to ask them about a variety of things that may have happened to them and to ask them about their perceptions of crime and conflict in society. This type of survey is a significant extension of victimization research, such as the National Crime Victimization Survey (NCVS), which identifies the extent and types of criminal victimization. While the NCVS gathers some information about situational factors and routine activities of respondents, victim surveys do not directly tap into the key concepts for operationalizing routine activities theory (see Meier and Miethe 1993), nor are these surveys designed to uncover factors that may explain the escalation of conflict to violence. Our study was designed to overcome these weaknesses. We use measures of conflict styles and lifestyle measures, addressing how conflict resolution mediates the impact of exposure to high-risk situations, thereby reducing the propensity to violence as a way of resolving conflict. In addition, we set out to redress the omissions of previous surveys that have paid little attention to the role of third parties (such as the police and legal profession) and the types and intensity of social networks (family, friends, and strangers). These can all play an important part in handling conflict, making it less likely to escalate to serious levels. This research represents an extension of our previous research on lifestyle and victimization processes (Kennedy and Forde 1990a, 1990b) and conflict management (Kennedy 1990). Following is a description of the social survey we conducted.[1]

The Study

We commissioned the Population Research Laboratory, University of Alberta, and the Winnipeg Area Study, University of Manitoba, to conduct a telephone survey of 2,052 persons in February and March 1994. These organizations use staffs of professional interviewers, supervisors, and data entry personnel to ensure a high level of quality in the data collection phase of the project. We designed the survey instrument and asked them to carry it out according to our specifications.

We selected a sample size of approximately 2,000 persons. Although it is much smaller than national victimization surveys, where sample sizes range from 50,000 to 70,000 persons, a sample of 2,000 permits an analysis of a wide range of types of conflict (e.g., from low to high in intensity). We expected, however, that this sample would not allow a detailed examination of specific types of conflict (e.g., disputes leading to aggravated assaults). Nonetheless, we expected to find a relatively high level of conflict and violence within the sample.

Manitoba and Alberta cover very large geographical areas, including three moderately large metropolitan areas and a vast rural mosaic. By drawing on samples of respondents from rural to metropolitan areas, we may uncover differences in social support networks that exist across these locations (Kennedy, Silverman, and Forde 1991). To reach persons throughout the region, we decided to use telephone interviewing[2] where we would interview one adult per household. The design is a two-stage sampling frame to obtain (1) a probability sample of households and (2) a predesignated selection of an adult respondent within each household to ensure an equal representation of male and female participants. Additional selection criteria were that respondents were eighteen years of age or older and that the dwelling unit was their usual place of residence.[3]

The statistical analysis uses a weighting procedure that translates differences in sample sizes to reflect the actual populations in each province and to take into account populations in the metropolitan areas and small cities and rural locales (see Appendix C). The objective in drawing a sample is for the survey to call upon enough people that we will be able to examine a wide range of conflict. At the same time, we would like to be able to reach out to a representative group from the population in a cost-efficient manner. The sampling procedures of the Population Research Laboratory and the Winnipeg Area Study permitted us to reach a representative population in each region.

We tested the quality of the survey through the analysis of refusals, interviewer assessments, and statistical assessment of selected variables. We base the acceptability of the refusal rate on the percentage of interviews that were completed in relation to the number of refusals, taking into account the survey research method. For telephone interviews, a response rate of 70 percent or higher is considered acceptable (Babbie 1989). This study achieved a very high overall response rate of 75 percent of eligible households. The average length of an interview was thirty-four minutes.

Rigorous interview protocols guaranteed a high response rate. If the interviewers were unsuccessful in establishing contact on their first call, they were to make at least ten callback attempts before declaring a telephone number as "no contact." Upon making contact, the interviewer identified herself or himself, verified the telephone number, and then asked the screening questions for selecting the respondent. Before administering the questionnaire, the interviewer advised the respondents that their participation was voluntary, that their responses would be kept completely confidential, and that they could stop the interview at any time. Approximately 20 percent of the respondents were recontacted by the supervisors for interviewing validation. No significant discrepancies or irregularities were found.

In social surveys we expect that some people will refuse to be interviewed. We asked interviewers to record information about all refusals on a refusal call sheet. These refusals were scrutinized by the supervisors to ascertain whether a second call should be made. Details of the refusal outlining the exact words used by the householder were recorded by the interviewers. In many cases, the refusal was not definite and final. Only the most experienced interviewers made callbacks to request an interview again and to explain further the purpose of the survey. More than one in three of the householders that were called back agreed to do an interview. Because of the high number of householders who agreed to an interview on a subsequent call, this recontacting procedure is a very worthwhile endeavor.

Interviewers also were required to evaluate the degree of cooperation of the respondents as well as the quality of the interview. Ninety-five percent of the respondents were judged as being cooperative, rather than indifferent or uncooperative. Ninety-eight percent of the interviews were assessed as being high quality or adequate, where quality refers to whether or not the respondents understood and responded to the questions. Ninety percent of respondents consented to allow the supervisor to call back, if required, for additional information. About 70 percent of respondents gave their full addresses so they would receive a copy of a survey highlights report.

A final test of the quality of the interviews was done where the characteristics of the sample are compared to information about the population as known from the Canadian Census. The Census is used as a baseline where the sample, if it is to be considered accurate, should look like the Census. A sociodemographic profile of the sample indicates the following facts: 51 percent are female; the median age is thirty-nine; about 60 percent are married or have a common-law marriage; 23 percent are single, 10 percent are divorced or separated, and 7 percent are widowed; 50 percent are employed full time; and 23 percent have less than a high school diploma, 25 percent have a high school diploma, 26 percent have completed some or all of a trade or technical school program, and 27 percent have completed some or all of a college degree. These numbers are representative of the target population, based on a comparison to the Census of Canada estimates in each province.

The Questions

We set out to examine how individuals will vary in their conflict management strategies depending on their orientations to violence, their understanding of acceptable interaction, and their lifestyles. In taking this perspective, we asked individuals to recount their orientations, behaviors, and interactions with others. A complete copy of the research instrument and the structure of the survey is provided in Appendix D. The major topics included the following:

- perceptions of crime and the criminal justice system
- approval of violence
- contact with police
- lifetime involvement in criminal victimization
- routine activities and lifestyle
- behavioral and perceptual information on actual interpersonal conflicts
- perceptual information on hypothetical conflicts
- risk-seeking behavior
- detailed sociodemographic information

We will address these topics in detail in the following chapters. In the rest of this chapter we will provide an overview of the results from questions that focused on the respondents' general experience with conflict and violence, as an introduction to the more detailed analyses that follow later.

Interpersonal Conflict in Society: An Overview

Felstiner (1974) suggests that most North Americans resolve interpersonal relations through avoidance. Is this true of all types of conflict? Do people use a common strategy or "routine" when dealing with a dispute? In chapter 3, we outlined a theoretical basis for understanding how conflict may be routinized. Here we will examine an array of types of conflict to test whether common strategies are used by people in dealing with different types of conflict.

It is true that not all interpersonal conflict results in serious crimes such as homicide, assault, robbery, theft, and burglary. Much conflict is expressed through less harmful disagreement. A neighbor may complain that the noise is too loud at a party in a neighborhood dispute. A husband may argue with his wife about the state of their family finances. People may disagree about which program to watch on television. In fact, we expect that conflicts may occur in many different situations. Thus, in order to study it in a systematic manner, we are forced to place some boundaries on where we will look.

The types of situations we defined as being important for study varied from incidents where crimes were committed or threats were made to interactions in public to family relations. The types of conflict could range from minor to serious. Based on studies of mediation, we assumed that courts are seen as a last resort in resolving disputes (Merry and Silbey 1984). Thus we developed a series of questions to explore the process of the development of disputes, including the effect that social relationships can have on the conflict.

We asked people about a number of forms of conflict[4] that they may have encountered. To put a temporal boundary on conflict, we asked people to talk about conflicts that they were involved in over the past year.

Everyone gets into conflicts with other people once in a while. Some disputes are very serious and some are not. I am going to ask you about some conflicts that you may have had with other adults (over eighteen) in the *last twelve months.*

In total, we examine seven different situations where respondents may have been involved in a conflict. The questions were designed so that respondents would include events that may have occurred in public or private. For example, people may have been involved in a street crime. Two of the conflicts were explicitly defined as being crimes against persons that may have been a completed criminal act (a robbery or an assault) or criminal threat. These questions closely parallel questions that would be found on a victimization survey. We also know from mediation studies (Merry and Silbey 1984), from research on family violence (e.g., Gelles and Straus 1988), and from research on the workplace (Lynch 1987) that many criminal acts of interpersonal violence occur in private locations. We designed questions that would ask about conflicts that occur in private situations. Finally, we used an open-ended question where respondents were asked to mention any other form of social conflict in which they were involved in the past year. As a whole, the questions allowed an estimation of the extent of social conflict experienced by our respondents.[5]

Experiences with Conflict

We asked people about their experiences with conflict over the past year. Table 4.1 shows the number of conflicts as responses, cases, and in the sample. The percentage of "responses" provides a breakdown in the distribution by the type of conflict. The percentage of "cases" provides an indication of the percentage of people involved in the type of conflict. The percentage of cases may add to more than 100, since people may have been involved in more than one type of conflict. The percentage of the sample is provided to illustrate how often a particular type of conflict occurs in the total population. Looking at the results by the type of conflict, we see that the most common type of dispute (30.5%) was an argument in the family reported by almost half (46.7%) of the respondents involved in a conflict. Second, many persons stated that they had had an argument over money (with family members or acquaintances). Table 4.1 also indicates that the least common form of conflict is a crime attack (robbery or assault), and that fewer people (3.6%) experienced a crime attack. A majority of the "other" conflict category involved disputes within the workplace. Overall, considering all types of conflict, about four in ten persons (42.8%) reported an involvement in some type of conflict in the past year.

Table 4.1
Experiences with Conflict in the Past Year

Types of Conflict	N	Responses (%)	Cases (%)	Sample (%)
Crime Attack	73	5.5	8.4	3.6
Threat of Crime Attack	135	10.1	15.4	6.6
Argument over Money	309	23.0	35.2	15.1
Argument with Landlord	78	5.8	8.9	3.8
Argument with Neighbor	112	8.3	12.7	5.4
Conflict with Family	410	30.5	46.7	20.0
Any Other Conflict	226	16.8	25.7	11.0
Any Conflict(s)	1344	100.0	153.0	42.8
No Conflicts	1172			57.2
Total Respondents	2050			100.0

A partial test of the validity of the items on conflict may be done by comparing these results to those from victimization surveys that ask about crime. An analysis that combines the responses to questions on crime attacks with the threat of crime attack shows that 9.1 percent of the sample from the current study were victims of a crime attack *or* the threat of a crime attack. This result is consistent with the 1981 victimization survey in Canada, where 6.3 percent of Canadians said they had been victims of actual (or attempted) robbery or assault (Solicitor General of Canada 1988) and the 1988 Canadian General Social Survey, which estimated that 8.3 percent of Canadians had been victims of a crime of personal violence.

Looking at the prevalence of conflict, Figure 4.1 shows that the majority (57%) of people said that they were not involved in any conflicts in the past year. Nonetheless, conflict is not a statistically rare event. On average, people were involved in 0.7 conflicts per person. For those respondents who said they were involved in at least one dispute, they most often were involved in only one incident. The average number of disputes for persons reporting at least one conflict was 1.5 disputes in the past year. A small number of persons, about 5 percent, reported that they were involved in three or more of the types of disputes we asked them about (Figure 4.1).

Explaining Conflict

We developed a series of questions to focus on the process of disputes, while recognizing that it would not be feasible to ask about every conflict. Following the lead questions about types of conflicts in the past year, we

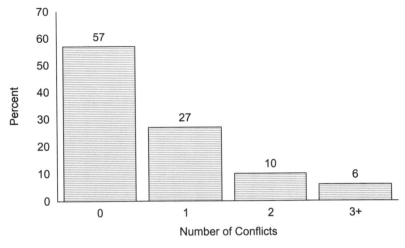

Figure 4.1
Total Number of Conflicts Reported in the Past Year

asked respondents to indicate which conflict was the *most serious* one. The definition of seriousness was left to the respondent. For those people who indicated only one form of conflict, the interviewers immediately moved to ask questions about it, where, for example, argument in your family would be probed as the specific incident.

I would like to ask you a few specific questions about the (state type of incident).

The information we will describe in this chapter focuses on the *most serious* incident, rather than all conflicts. This procedure permits a larger number of questions about a specific incident and eases the burden on respondents of repetitive questions about each type of incident.

Figure 4.2 shows the distribution of the most serious conflict for people in the past year. The pattern within the figure closely approximates the distribution of responses for all conflicts reported in the past year. This information includes cases where only one conflict was reported. Conflicts in the family and arguments over money were most often rated as being the most serious conflict in the past year. Disputes with landlords and neighbors were of low prevalence. Interestingly, crime attacks and threats of a crime attack were not always selected as the most serious conflict when more than one conflict was reported. As would be expected, crime attacks were selected over threats of crime, but in several instances family-based conflicts were chosen as the most serious conflict when compared to crime attacks or

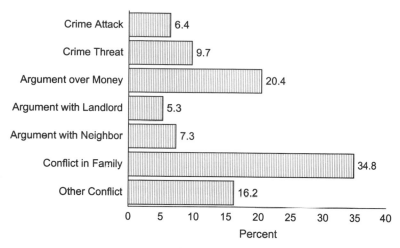

Figure 4.2
Most Serious Conflict in the Past Year

threats of crime. Looking at open-ended responses drawn from the next question in the survey, several people indicated that they made this selection because of the longer duration of the relationship between disputants (husband–wife, sibling, and so on) and the expectation of a continued relationship. For example, a respondent said

> I am related to them, it was not going away until resolved. I'll forget about the stranger at the bar but not my brother.

Selection of the most serious conflict in the past year yields sufficient data for a study of conflict in society across a variety of situations. Bear in mind that we use relatively broad classifications of types of conflict, because some of its forms are relatively rare events.

Seriousness of Conflict and Violence

To determine the perceived severity of events, we asked respondents to rate the seriousness of the conflict on a Likert scale where a score of "1" was not at all serious and "7" was extremely serious. The questionnaire was designed to cover a variety of situations, with the severity of conflict ranging from trivial to serious. For example, it is reasonable to expect that persons involved in crime and crime threats would rate these as serious events. Note that we are not asking individual respondents to rate different types of conflict,

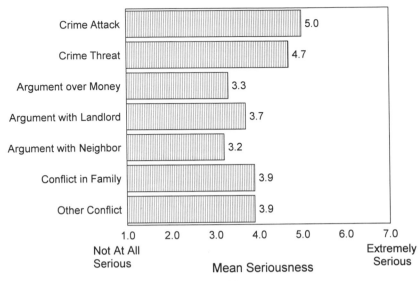

Figure 4.3
Seriousness of Conflict by Situation

but that we are asking different respondents about different forms of conflict.

Figure 4.3 suggests that the prevalence of crime attacks and crime threats were rated as the most serious type of conflicts, as they received the highest average ratings. In contrast, arguments with neighbors were given the lowest score. Conflicts in the family and arguments over money also were rated, on average, as low to moderate. The overall rating of seriousness for all types of conflict was 3.5 out of 7, with a standard deviation of 1.9. This suggests that the disputes people told us about in the interviews were, on average, of low to moderate severity.

An analysis of the distribution of severity for each of the types of conflict indicates that crimes and crime threats were more likely to be seen as serious but that some people ranked crimes or crime threats as trivial events. The distribution of family conflicts differed from this pattern, as most events were seen as low to moderate in seriousness but some were seen as extreme. It is important to note this variation, since we will show later that seemingly trivial events can escalate to more extreme forms of violence.

Another measure of the seriousness of a dispute is whether or not violence was used in the dispute. Rather than asking people what they thought about the seriousness of the dispute—an attitudinal measure—we questioned them whether people were struck, hurt, or injured—a behavioral measure.[6]

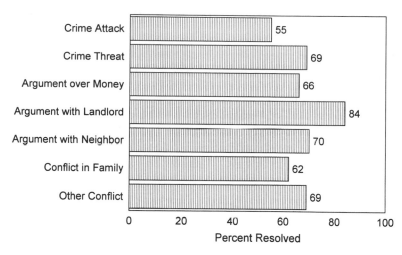

Figure 4.4
Resolution of Conflict

Results indicate that 13 percent of conflicts involved some degree of violence. Violence was equally likely whether males or females were involved. Young persons were more likely than older persons to report the occurrence of violence as part of their most serious conflict.

Dispute Resolution

Did people resolve their disputes? We asked people this question directly, and if the dispute was resolved, how did they do this? Figure 4.4 shows that there is a high degree of variation regarding whether disputes were resolved. Patterns indicate that they are least likely to be resolved if they involved a crime attack and most likely to be dealt with if they were a landlord–tenant dispute. Notably, a large proportion of family disputes remain unresolved. Correlational analysis shows that the likelihood of resolution of a dispute increases as the seriousness of the dispute decreases. A limitation of these data is that we only asked respondents about the most serious conflict in the past year, so the actual number of resolved conflicts would be lower that what we report here, since less serious disputes remain unresolved.

Overall, it is important to note that a strong majority, two in three, of conflicts were resolved. Resolution, nonetheless, depends on the type and seriousness of the dispute.

Demographic Factors

The relationships between conflict and demographic factors such as gender, age, marital status, education, and income were evaluated. The results indicate that the proportion of men and women involved in conflict is about equal. Males and females reported similar levels of involvement across the different types of conflict, with the exception of conflict in the family, where females indicated more conflict than males (41 percent versus 29 percent) for the past year. The greatest single demographic factor for predicting involvement in conflict is a person's age. Younger persons, particularly those aged eighteen to thirty-four, were much more likely than older persons to report involvement in conflict. Age is related to the type of conflict as well, with younger persons more likely to have a dispute with a landlord and younger persons also more likely than older persons to be involved in crime attacks and crime threats. Other demographic factors such as marital status (other than persons who were divorced), household income, and education did not have a great influence on the number of conflicts that people were involved in during the past year.

Recall from earlier in this chapter that violence was used in 13 percent of disputes. The use of violence in a dispute does not appear to be related to gender. Males and females were equally likely to report experience with violence in their most serious conflict. Again, note that we do not have a measure of the severity of the extent of violence that is known to differ by gender. The use of violence in disputes was significantly related to age, with younger persons much more likely to report the occurrence of violence. Social factors appear to have influenced the dispute process. Violence was much more likely to occur when a third party was said to have started the dispute.

Summary

The concept of interpersonal conflict in society is relatively broad. Traditional sources about crime do not collect much information about what led to the escalation of conflict into violence and crime. This study used a survey research method to gather information about interpersonal conflict. We have provided an overview of the questions that we used in the survey, described some of the features of conflict, and identified some of the limitations of the research.

While this study did not attempt to classify all possible variations of types of conflict, it has identified the extent to which people may face conflict in their daily lives. We found that at least four in ten people were involved in some type of conflict in the past year. The seriousness of these conflicts ranged from trivial to very serious, with the severity of most incidents rated by respondents as low to moderate. The chapter also discusses how the emergence and progression of disputes and dispute resolution can be influenced by demographic and social factors, particularly age. Given that the majority of disputes were of low seriousness, it is not surprising that few respondents called upon a formal response from the criminal justice system or through litigation.

We also have provided a brief discussion about how the results of this study may be compared to victimization surveys as a means to assess the reliability and validity of our measures of conflict. We found that the extent of conflict in society, using questions about crime attacks and crime threats, was consistent with results from victimization surveys. The similarity of these findings is important because it gives us confidence that the results of this study will generalize to society. Similar to findings from victimization surveys about reporting crime to the police, the results from this study showed that much conflict is resolved and that only a small amount of conflict involved the criminal justice system.

In chapters 5 and 6 we will conduct a more detailed analysis of the process of dispute resolution in an attempt to understand crime and conflict in society. We know that a large number of people solve disputes and crime on their own. We will look to the steps people take before deciding to involve formal agencies, such as the police, in crime and conflict. With this information, we may be better prepared to understand, and possibly prevent, the escalation of conflict into crime.

Chapter 5

⊸◈⊸

Attitudes Toward Violence: Setting Up Routines

Introduction

Descriptions of violent criminal events are reported in prominent places in the news media every day. There are many questions surrounding such events. Did they begin as arguments? Did the offender know the other people? Were drugs and alcohol involved? Were the guns legal? Did the victim have a gun too? Was he a member of a gang? Could someone have done something to stop the killing? We want to know what we can do to stop or control violence, and also to understand its causes.

Criminologists (e.g., Wolfgang and Ferracuti 1967) have used the concept of subculture to explain higher crime rates where belief systems, associated with values that could be described as violent, were shown to be related to the level of the violence that occurs in society. Subcultural theorists have attempted to explain demographic variations in violence. For example, violent crime in the American South often is attributed to a Southern *subculture of violence* (Gastil 1971), and homicide in Western Canada is related to the violent undercurrents of living in the *Wild West* (see Kennedy, Silverman, and Forde 1991). The major proposition of these subcultural studies is that belief systems may legitimate the use of crime and violence in society. Most researchers that have attempted to test this theory (e.g., Gastil 1971; Hackney 1969) have used indirect measures of values to examine the relationship of subculture with violent crime, while attributing subculture to membership in the group, such as living in the American South, assuming that a person is subject to a Southern subculture of violence (Dixon and Lizotte 1987).

Legitimization of Violence in Society

A stronger and more direct measure of people's values was developed by Ball–Rokeach (1973), who designed a number of questions to test the relationship between values and violence. These questions have been asked of people in the United States in national surveys on a regular basis since 1973 (see McGuire, Pastore, and Flanagan 1995). People were queried about whether they would approve of the use of violence if an adult male stranger or (in another set a questions) a male police officer was hitting a person in a particular situation.

Ball–Rokeach designed these questions to identify the extent to which people hold a value that supports the approval of violence. Are these measures valid? Results of national surveys that use the Ball–Rokeach scale are readily available to the public, as reported annually in the Sourcebook of Criminal Justice Statistics (McGuire et al. 1995). Recently, researchers have chosen to focus on a subset of the questions, items about police use of force, using them in their discussions of public opinion about police use of excessive force (Ross 1995). Erlanger (1975) and Lynch and Danner (1993) challenge the validity of the Ball–Rokeach questions, arguing that the questions are too artificial. For example, the questions only deal with instances that involve adult males who are strangers. As such, they argue, the items will not inform us about instances where people know each other, which is where much violence occurs. The questions also do not vary the level of intensity of the violence, for example, does it not matter if it is a hit that makes a person bleed?

Dixon and Lizotte (1987) argue that the Ball–Rokeach questions about the legitimization of violence may represent separate constructs: offensive (violent) attitudes; defensive attitudes toward violence and aggression; and a residual category that is neither offensive nor defensive. In some of the situations, there is a degree of legitimacy for the use of aggressive behavior. We agree with this assessment of the scale. Thus we will examine relationships of violent and defensive attitudes with crime and conflict. This chapter assesses the extent that people will legitimate the use of violence by *others* and by *themselves*. We expect that the *legitimate use* of violence can affect the extent of *illegitimate and criminal* violence in society (Straus 1985). We can use this assessment as a way of identifying the major components of social constructionist theory as it relates to the definition of violence and conflict in society.

Accepting the weaknesses, we chose to include the Ball–Rokeach items (Table 5.1) in the present study as standardized questions, since they have been used in a number of surveys. In doing so, we may compare the results of this study with previous research. We do, however, agree with Dixon and Lizotte (1987) that the items represent separate constructs for offensive violence, defensive violence, and neither offensive nor defensive attitudes.

Table 5.1
Items Used to Construct Violent and Defensive Attitude Scales

Suppose you are a witness to an incident where one man punches an adult male stranger.

Would you approve if the adult stranger

A.	. . . was in a protest march showing opposition to the other man's views?	Violent attitude
B.	. . . was drunk and bumped into the man and his wife on the street?	Violent attitude
C.	. . . had hit the man's child after the child accidentally damaged the stranger's car?	Defensive attitude
D.	. . . was beating up a woman *and* the man saw it?	Defensive attitude
E.	. . . had broken into the man's house?	Defensive attitude

Next, would you approve of a police officer striking an adult male citizen

F.	. . . if the male citizen had said vulgar and obscene things to the police officer?	Violent attitude
G.	. . . if the male citizen was being questioned as a suspect in a murder case?	Violent attitude
H.	. . . if the male citizen was attempting to escape from custody?	Neither violent nor defensive
I.	. . . if the male citizen was attacking the police officer with his fists?	Neither violent nor defensive

Notes: Respondents refusing to answer, or uncertain were excluded from the analysis.
1 = Yes; 0 = No.

Ninety-four percent of people said they would approve of violence in at least one of the nine situations defined by Ball–Rokeach. This is an indication that there is a near universal value for a tolerance of the legitimacy of some form of violence in society. People will legitimate some violence, but how much violence, and under what circumstances? We find that respondents would approve of violence in about one in three of the situations ($\bar{x} = 3.3$, s = 1.7). The results also show clear situational differences, in Figure 5.1, as most persons would legitimate the use of violence if a police officer was hitting an adult male who was attempting to escape from custody, or where a man was attacking a police officer with his fists. However, few people would approve of violence where a

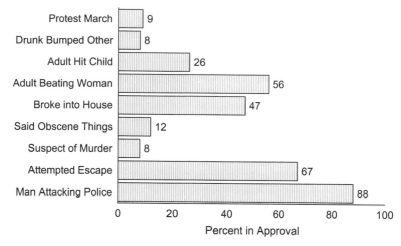

Figure 5.1
Approval of Violence by Situation

drunk bumped into a man and his wife, or where a man had said obscene things to a police officer. Also, very few people would approve of violence where police officers would be free to strike a man being questioned as a suspect in a murder case. The patterns in the descriptive results of approval of violence from this study are remarkably consistent with findings of a U.S. national study conducted in 1994 (See tables in McGuire et al. 1995). Western Canadians and Americans may share similar values about the social construction of violence.

Additional analysis of overall approval of violence from the current study was used to assess its relation to sex, age, education, and income. We find that males are more likely to approve of violence than are females. Approval does not vary with age. There is a weak relation between approval of violence and education, where persons with a higher education are less likely to approve of violence. There is no association between income and approval of violence.

A factor analysis of the information from the current study shows that these items clearly break into the three factors suggested by Dixon and Lizotte (1987). About 25 percent of the people answering the survey indicated that they would approve of using at least one of the four violent attitude items ($\bar{x} = 0.4$; s = 0.7). Two in three people, a much greater proportion compared to violent attitudes, would approve of at least one form of defensive use of violence ($\bar{x} = 1.3$; s = 1.1). In fact, there is near universal support for police use of force in situations where a prisoner is attempting to escape or is hitting the officer, with 91 percent of people in approval of violence on at least one of the two items ($\bar{x} = 1.6$; s = 0.7).

Dixon and Lizotte restricted their analysis to male respondents. This study examines a general population that allows us to make some additional comparisons across social groups looking at these three factors. We find that males are more likely than females to hold more violent and more defensive attitudes in the approval of violence. Consistent with Dixon and Lizotte, we find a positive relation between violent attitudes and age and a negative relation between defensive attitudes and age. Violent attitudes also are inversely related to education and income, so persons with a higher education and higher income are less likely to hold beliefs in the approval of violence. Defensive attitudes were not related to education or income. Neither the violent nor the defensive attitudes were related to geographical location, which we coded as metropolitan versus rural.

The subculture of violence thesis predicts a direct relationship between the approval of violence and the level of criminality in society. We asked people if they had ever been arrested and what the arrest was about. These open-ended responses are coded into five categories: 89.0 % said they had not ever been arrested (0), 2.8% reported a misdemeanor (1), 4.8% indicated a drug or an alcohol offense (2), 1.7% were arrested for a property crime (3), and 1.6% said they had been arrested for a person crime (4). As we would expect, more males and younger persons reported more arrests, and people with a lower level of education indicated more arrests than did persons with higher levels of education. We find that there is no relation between violent or defensive beliefs and the type of arrest. However, there is a weak relationship between defensive beliefs and whether or not a person has been arrested.

Constructing Disputes through Language

Our concern about the ways in which people define what is acceptable or not can be taken from the general attitudes they express about the legitimacy of violence to specific responses they make about what they expect that they would do in certain circumstances. The evolution of disputes involve participants applying labels to their actions, including justifications and explanations of other people's actions, including blame. The articulation of this interaction relies on the depiction of action through language. Conflict, then, becomes a social construct in which *facts* are ordered and *norms* are invoked in particular ways, "ways that reflect the personal interests or values of the participant or that anticipate the definitions offered by others" (Mather and Yngvesson 1980–1981). Understanding the language of disputes is most critical in situations where legal codes and legal discourse are employed. Mather and Yngvesson report that the subculture of the criminal court routinely modifies the categories of crime to produce working definitions of *normal crime* and *real criminals*. Black (1983) reinforces this point when he discusses criminal cases arising out of quarrels and fights, where each party has a grievance against the other. The state imposes the categories of offender and victim upon people who are contesting the proper application of these labels during the altercation.

Further, because of the dichotomized nature of criminal law, acts become right or wrong (non-crimes or crimes) and persons become noncriminals or criminals (Christie 1986). Fundamentally, penal law looks more into acts than into interactions. This removes the negotiated feature of civil disputes from criminal ones. The narrowing and expanding of disputes is dependent, then, on language that defines the grievance and categorizes the nature of the conflict. There is an important insight here, especially when we consider this problem in the context of definitions of violence and the role disputes have in affecting the evolution to crime. There may, in fact, not be a change in the behavior. Rather, a judgment can be made that the dispute will be best dealt with as criminal through a narrowing process. Alternatively, a criminal act may be expanded to illustrate the grievance of the actors and justified in terms of saving property, face, or principle, factors addressed through the use of coercive action (Kennedy 1990).

For Luckenbill and Doyle (1989), the key concepts for understanding disputes are naming, claiming, and aggression.[1] In the evolution of the dispute through naming, blaming, and claiming, the focus of the dispute becomes more defined through a narrowing of issues (Mather and Yngvesson 1980–1981). Narrowing further emphasizes the importance of the social construction of the dispute process. Naming involves recognition by an individual of a negative outcome from someone else's behavior (Felstiner et al. 1980–1981). For example, a person sees that another person has cut in front of him or her in a line at the movie theater. For naming to be present, the person must notice that the interaction has taken place. Without recognition of the situation as a conflict, the situation cannot be named as a potential conflict.

Claiming requires that the individual express a demand for reparation, an explicit need to pursue some form of coercion to redress a hurt or to punish another. Claiming is required for a situation to escalate into a dispute. This occurs when a person names and claims but the potential harm doer rejects the victim's claim. Claiming is a situated process where the actions of both the victim and offender come into conflict. However, situations need not escalate into a dispute, as either the victim or the offender may recognize the other's claim in a situation.

It is at the claiming stage that the selection of *routine conflict* processes takes place. The decision to go forward and escalate the conflict or to back off is made here. A quick assessment must be made about the consequences of this decision. It is at this stage that many people will stop the interaction. But, on later reflection, they may feel that they should have acted differently. The elements of bravado, the *quick quip* that would have wounded the other and scored points, are recreated in the aftermath of this decision. Of course, this is stored away to be used at a different time and a different place when similar circumstances appear. As in the case of the multiple offender homicides described by Cheatwood (1996), the first or second encounter may not lead to a lethal outcome. But the murder occurs when the individuals go through with their rehearsed grievance, dispatching the victim for past wrongs and settling unsettled claims.

The third and final stage in the model is aggression. Luckenbill and Doyle (1989) suggest that this may be studied by looking at aggressiveness, which ". . . is defined as the willingness of the individual to persevere and use force to settle the dispute" (p. 423). Disputes also can be solved in a variety of ways. These include going to the police, bringing other parties into the dispute to act as mediators, or simply withdrawing from the situation. The extent to which people reach aggression is affected by the structural position of the disputants, definitions of the situations (including goal setting), and third party actions. These factors combine into what Luckenbill and Doyle explain as the predisposition to escalate the dispute. Strategies for aggression may be used routinely as a way of winning conflict situations and getting one's way— a form of rational choice in conflict situations.

As part of our research, we included what is called a factorial survey as part of our study instrument.[2] While we would like to examine conflict in an as wide-ranging scope as possible, in a social survey respondent burden is an issue when a large number of situations (questions on the survey) are to be considered because of the time constraints of an interview. Rossi and Nock (1982) suggest that this problem may be overcome through the use of a factorial survey. In a factorial survey, a random sample of types of scenarios are assigned to respondents who themselves are randomly assigned within each experimental condition. The aim of the factorial design is to provide an evaluation of individual level differences within each scenario and to examine the consensus across types of scenarios.

A strength of a factorial survey design is that a wider variety of social situations may be presented to respondents than they would encounter in their daily lives. Situations vary from routine or mundane conflicts to rarer forms of criminal violence. Factorial surveys are heavily dependent on the a priori assumptions of investigators of the types of dimensions that they will include in the factorial design (Lynch and Danner 1993).

Using hypothetical situations of conflict, intensity varies from mundane to rarer forms of criminal violence. Thus we can assess the extent to which people say they would use routine conflict approaches in the legitimization of

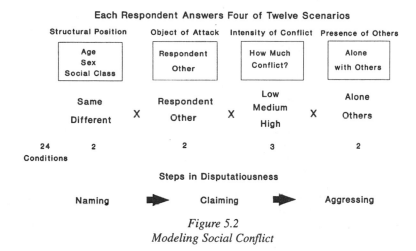

Figure 5.2
Modeling Social Conflict

aggression. Respondents were shown varying circumstances and intensities of conflicts. The escalation of dispute outcomes also varies along several dimensions: the position of the harm doer relative to the respondent; the degree to which the individual appears under attack; and the setting of the interaction. The use of a standardized set of vignettes, in an experimental design, permits an analysis of the conditional effects of each of these variables. It also improves on designs of previous studies of the propensity toward violence, replacing questions that asked people to imagine situations in which violence would be used (Ball–Rokeach 1973), as we described in the previous section, with scenarios where people are asked for their responses to set questions related to their actions in routine situations.

In a factorial survey, a wide variety of settings can be selected for the modeling of disputes. At issue is whether or not it is possible to develop a series of realistic scenarios probing key factors that may influence how interpersonal relations escalate from low-level conflict to aggression. Each scenario must be designed to isolate the predisposition toward taking the steps from naming to claiming to aggressiveness. The extent to which these elements constitute a high or low intensity of routine conflict provides us with the bases upon which to focus on particular groups and situations that engender certain styles of behavior.

We developed twelve scenarios for use in a factorial survey of the legitimization of aggression. These were sorted so that there were three scenarios in each of the workplace, street, family, and leisure domains. Within each scenario, a parallel series of specific questions was used in the factorial design, illustrated in Figure 5.2, which included twenty-four different conditions permitting the manipulation of the structural position, object of attack, intensity of conflict, and presence of others. One scenario was randomly selected from each domain of conflict. The advantage of presenting only four scenarios to each respondent is that it allows a wider number of scenarios to be administered while maintaining subsample sizes to perform an analysis of each type of conflict. There is a random assignment of all of the conditions within each scenario, and all of the scenarios use the same basic factorial design.

To administer the factorial survey, we printed a copy of all of the possible combinations in each of the twelve scenarios. Next, we scrambled the order of attributes in each set by shuffling the paper. Third, a random numbers table was used to select one scenario from each of the four domains, four scenarios in all, for each questionnaire. Fourth, we printed five copies of the randomly ordered scenario sets so that we would have enough copies of scenarios for 2,400 completed interviews. Finally, the scenarios were inserted and stapled into the complete questionnaire.

For example, the public school scenario was structured as follows:

Suppose (you/you and a friend) are walking across a field at a public school in late afternoon. The school yard is (practically empty/very crowded). A (male/female) (lower class/middle class/wealthy) looking (youth/person in their thirties/elderly person) (tells [you/your friend]/ yells insulting comments at [you/your friend]/ pushes at [you/your friend]) to get you off of the field.

In reading the scenario, a female respondent may be the object of attention, where a potential harm doer tells her to get off of the field. We can assess whether she would react differently if the attack was against her or someone else. Would she react differently if it is a male or female who is about to harm her? The sex of the potential harm doer may be manipulated reading the descriptor *male* or *female*. The age of the potential harm doer is manipulated to look at differences in structural position for youth, an elderly person, and a person in his or her thirties. We also wanted to know if the intensity of the conflict made a difference. We expected that intensity would matter, but we also wondered if a low-intensity attack would be enough for a person to push back in one situation and not enough for them to do so in another situation. The factorial design enabled us to test many possibilities. Remember though that only one descriptor is used in a scenario that is presented to a respondent. The experiment controls for differences in presentation to subjects as the attributes for each of the possible manipulations of variables were randomly assigned to respondents. People did not have a choice about which types of situations in the scenarios they would encounter. The complete set of scenarios is included as Appendix E.

Explaining Naming, Claiming, and Aggression

For each scenario, a standardized set of closed-ended questions is used to evaluate naming, claiming, and aggressing. There are different ways of making an assessment of whether people recognize a negative outcome. For example, we could ask people whether or not the incident would be a problem. At the same time, we wanted to know how much of a problem the incident would be for them. Is it routine? Is it serious? Other studies used a measurement of how upset people are with a crime as a measure of the extent that people view crime as a serious outcome (Cox and Collins 1985). We asked people how upset they would be with a potential harm doer to assess the degree that they would *name* the situation as a potential dispute operationalized by asking the following question immediately after describing the scenario:

On a scale from 0 to 10, how upset would you be with this person? ("0" being not at all upset and "10" being extremely upset.)

Not at all upset   Extremely upset

0 1 2 3 4 5 6 7 8 9 10

We consider any number greater than "0" to be an indication that people *name* the situation as one in which they are in conflict with the potential harm doer. There is an implicit assumption in the causal process of making a dispute that people must engage in *naming* before they may move to *claiming*. If people do not see something as a problem, we would not expect them to make a claim.

Questions on claiming and aggression are next, with each question tailored to match the scenario's intensity of conflict, the sex of the potential harm doer, and the object of attack. For example, claiming may be operationalized as follows:

Would you tell him to mind his own business?

Yes . . . 1

No . . . 2

A yes or no response was used, since we are only interested in whether or not the respondent informs the potential harm doer that he or she does not want him or her to continue his or her actions. The convergence of naming and claiming meets the criteria for an engagement in a dispute. Some of the disputes will be trivial and others will be severe. Assignment of types of disputes to the subjects is random, so we can analyze whether people use a common pattern in dealing with disputes.

Last, for persons who make claims, we asked them about the use of aggression. We assume that people who will not make a claim will not pursue interaction with the potential harm doer. Subjects who do not make a claim are assumed to have left the situation or are avoiding interaction with the other person. Aggression is measured as follows:

If the person continued to yell at you, would you use physical force to make them stop?

Yes . . . 1
No . . . 2

A definition of what constitutes physical force was left up to the respondent. We are interested in any physical action of aggressing they would take to stop the potential harm doer. Of course, some acts will be more serious than others. We can estimate the severity by looking at the intensity of the conflict, assuming that more intense conflicts will require more intense responses. A greater concern is that people may say they will do things but not really do them. The reliability and validity of aggression in hypothetical situations is assessed by comparing these results to what people report for their actual instances of conflict and by comparing them to results of victimization surveys. An open-ended question also is included for people who say they will use physical force when we ask if there is anything that would stop them from using physical force in the situation. This helps us understand how people see the situation and what types of things may act as deterrents to violence.

Independent Variables

We would like to know what kinds of things may explain why people will be upset, make claims, or legitimate the use of aggression. The independent variables are shown in Figure 5.3. We can look at whether the respondent is the object of attack, or whether it was another person in the scenario. The intensity of conflict is operationalized as low, medium, or high.[3] Finally, the presence of others is set up to describe the respondent as if he or she is alone, or with others.

Luckenbill and Doyle (1989) argue that previous theories of structural position and violence have yielded inconsistent and contradictory findings, because they have ignored situational factors that may intervene in the processes that lead to the escalation of disputes. "These theories focus on why certain people are more disposed to violence than others, but they do not specify the situational conditions that channel such dispositions into concrete lines of actions" (p. 422).

So, depending on how individuals relate to one another, the interaction will differ despite the fact that the circumstances of the event may appear the same. For example, a contest of wills between two young men in a bar over a topic of disagreement may lead to quite different consequences than the same argument between a young man and woman. We are conscious of our social standing relative to others, and we use these as cues in governing our behavior toward one another.

What do we know about the relationship between individuals' placement in the social structure and aggression? Research shows that young men engage in an overwhelming majority of crimes of violence (Wilson and Herrnstein 1985). Lower-income groups have higher rates of violence than do middle- and upper-income groups (Messner 1982). Age, income, race, and region are strong predictors of homicide (Nelsen, Corzine, and Huff–Corzine 1994). Knowing who offenders are, though, is not enough to predict the escalation of conflict. This points to the importance of the circumstances in daily interaction that stimulate aggressive action. The remainder of this chapter demonstrates how a factorial model using scenarios of situations, where people are placed in conflict with a potential harm doer, may be used to identify pathways to aggression and violence.

Luckenbill and Doyle (1989) suggest that conflict is more likely to escalate if people are of the same structural position. The structural position of the harm doer in the scenarios is evaluated in terms of whether he or she is the same as or different from the respondent. Of all the experimental conditions, structural position is most difficult to administer, since it consists of manipulations of age, sex, and social class characteristics. Since the sex of the respondent was not known prior to each interview, the structural position variables are analytically identified using characteristics of the respondents compared to descriptions of the potential harm doers in the scenarios. The structural position variables were classified as the same or different than the potential harm doer. To complete this procedure, the age of respondents was grouped as 18 to 34, 35 to 64, and 65 and over. The household income of respondents also was grouped in three categories, using the Census of Canada definition of low income as a guide: less than $30,000, $30,000 to 59,000, or $60,000 or more. These income categories were compared to the scenario descriptions of low-, middle- and wealthy-looking persons.

Analytic and Control Variables

Several analytic and control variables were included in the scenarios. The sex and age of the harm doer (eighteen years old, thirty-five years old, or elderly) were indicated. Also, the social class of the protagonist was identified

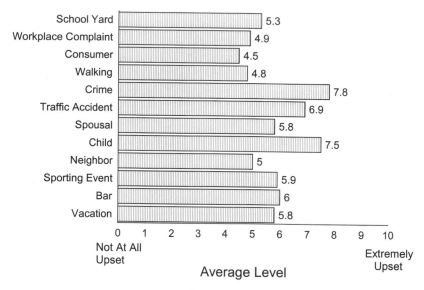

Figure 5.3
Level of Upset with a Potential Harm Doer by Scenario

as a lower-class looking, middle-class looking, or wealthy-looking person.

Household income has the highest rate of nonresponse in the survey (25% either refused or did not know). Nonetheless, income is included in the analysis, with listwise deletion of cases, because income is necessary for identifying the structural position of respondents relative to other persons in the scenarios.

Descriptive Analysis of Naming, Claiming, and Aggression

One of the necessary conditions for a person to enter into a dispute is that he or she must *name* the actions of the potential harm doer as being against his or her own interests. The scenarios place the respondent in what would be a face-to-face conflict with a potential harm doer. We assess the likelihood of naming by asking people how upset they would be with the actions of the potential harm doer. Results of the factorial survey suggest that there are situational differences, in the likelihood that people would name the actions of a potential harm doer as a negative action. This is evident, looking at an average upset response evaluated across each of the experimental conditions. Figure 5.3 illustrates that people are more likely to be upset with a potential harm doer in street scenarios and less likely to be upset in workplace scenarios. The average level of upset with the potential disputant, for our sam-

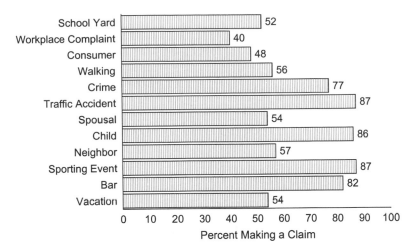

Figure 5.4
Claims Against a Harm Doer by Scenario

ple, is 5.9 out of 10. Finding a moderate degree of upset using the scenarios is an indication that people recognize that they would be in conflict with a potential harm doer in the scenario. Of course, as standard deviations indicate, there also is some variation in the level of upset for each scenario.

Respondents indicate that they would make a claim, where they would ask the potential harm doer to stop, in 65 percent of the scenarios. Figure 5.4 shows situational differences with a high degree of variation in when people will make a claim against the other. Claims are less often made in workplace disputes and more often pursued in street disputes. There also is a moderate degree of variation in the likelihood of claiming in each domain.

Respondents said that they would use force against a potential harm doer to get them to stop in 15 percent of the conflicts. Figure 5.5 clearly shows that the use of aggression varies substantially by situation, as it would very rarely be chosen if used against neighbors but it would often be selected against a potential harm doer in a crime. People also say that they would use force in about one in five of the household situations involving a spouse or child. Remarkable in these findings is the fact that people in workplace situations, when faced with an irate customer who assaults them, are highly unlikely to respond in kind, while in crime situations this aggression is highly likely. Individuals do not exhibit different levels of aggressive tendencies, then, but rather are highly constrained by their views of circumstance and consequence. When these results concerning workplace behavior were discussed with an undergraduate class (many members of which work part time),

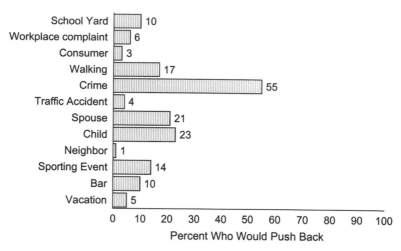

Figure 5.5
Aggression Against a Potential Harm Doer by Scenario

there was a general consensus that this is how they would act (that is, they would restrain themselves from responding to violent customers with violence), since they would be afraid of losing their jobs. The crime scenario makes the concern about consequences quite different, allowing for a more proactive response without fear of being punished for this violent action. As we will see, when we look at the ways in which street youth respond to these scenarios, as discussed in chapter 7, the situational determinants seem to have a strong effect on setting up violent repertoires.

These averages for level of upset, claiming, and use of aggression should not be taken as representative of the averages for each in real-life situations, since dimensions in the factorial model were assigned in equal numbers in the scenarios (e.g., equal numbers of low-, medium-, and high-intensity conflicts of which we expect that high intensity would be rarer events).[4] However, the averages do allow an examination of how and why people would deal with conflict in different domains and situations. Using a factorial survey, we have identified variation in the dependent variables—the extent to which people would be upset, make claims, or use aggression—and we would like to know what can explain it. Is it the intensity of the dispute? Do the age and sex of the disputants make a difference? Is it the structural position of the disputants? Do people call the police? What will stop them from using aggression? The factorial survey allows us to examine a wide variety of factors that may influence the pathways to aggression.

Multivariate Analysis of Naming, Claiming, and Aggression

Data limitations and a lack of empirical work done on the dynamics of conflict have hampered the ability to study the relationship between conflict escalation and aggression. Multivariate analysis using a factorial survey overcomes many of the difficulties encountered in the literature on aggression and violence. It allows us to look at a range of conflicts for an assessment of the stability of characteristics across types of disputes. Rather than looking at one type of conflict and comparing it to features that may be seen in another type of conflict, a factorial design takes common elements from a variety of disputes and pools the data enabling a statistical test of whether a situated transaction has a routine character when people engage in interpersonal conflicts. Additionally, the factorial model allows us to assess how differences in response in conflict can be attributed to situational differences (differences based on a particular scenario).

In setting the stage to examine the results of the factorial survey, recall that we expect people will routinize aspects of the dispute process so that naming, claiming, and aggression will be predictable under certain conditions. Nonetheless, based on propositions of social constructionist theories, we expect that people will bring different expectations into different situations. Some situations will engender different expectations, so that they are more upsetting than others, claims are more often made, and aggression is more often used. A factorial model allows an experimental manipulation of features of the dispute and a test of the routine conflict theory of violence.

The following results are based on data that is pooled, so that all twelve of the scenarios may be examined together and analyzed using regression and logistic regression to estimate the effects of structural position, demographic characteristics, and situational factors on naming (upset), claiming, and aggression. Situational differences are estimated using deviation coding rather than dummy variable coding, with coefficients representing a comparison of the particular situation to the average for all situations (see Menard 1995).[5] Ordinary least squares regression is used for level of upset, since it is an interval level variable (coded 0 = not at all upset to 10 = very much). Logistic regression is used to examine claiming (1 = yes, 0 = no) and aggression (1 = yes, 0 = no), as they are nominal level variables.

Table 5.2 presents the results of the regression analyses. As we begin to go through the pooled regression analysis, think about the dispute as though we were looking at the transaction phase of the event. If there is a routine character in disputes we should find a direct relationship between the intensity of conflict and whether people get upset, how often they will make claims, and if they would use aggression against a potential harm doer. Those who name are expected to more often make a claim, and those who make a claim will more often use aggression in disputes. Indeed, the results in Table 5.2 indicate a moderate and direct relationship between the level of upset and the intensity of the conflict. This suggests that people routinize the naming of conflict, so as the intensity of the conflict increases, they will more likely see it as a potentially harmful event.

While there is an overall statistical relationship between the intensity of conflict and naming, as measured by level of upset, it also is important to look at the situation. Looking further down Table 5.2 to the estimates of deviation coefficients for the scenarios, we have a statistical assessment of how much each scenario differs from the mean for all of the scenarios. For example, the direction and magnitude of the coefficients tells us that people are less upset in the convenience store scenario and much more upset in the crime scenario than the average for all disputes. Stepping back to a simpler analysis of means by the intensity of conflict, Figure 5.6 reports how upset people would be if they were walking down the street to a convenience store and were confronted by another. In this scenario, there is a direct relationship between the intensity of the conflict and how upset people get. That is, people get more upset as the intensity of the harm increases. As Figure 5.7 shows, however, people confronted with street crime tend to be upset irrespective of the intensity of the conflict in the situation. If the scenarios really are covering the spectrum of social conflict, we would expect that people would *name* any robbery a conflict. They do, in fact, as 39 percent of people rate robbery as "extremely problematic" and only 2 percent relate that it would be "not at all" a problem. This also is reflected in the average level of upset for the crime scenario, which is higher in all conditions than even the high-intensity condition for the walking scenario. While we expect people will learn how to deal with conflict, from the differing intensities of conflict, a repertoire for dealing with it does not necessitate that people see differing levels of intensity in a coercive situation such as a robbery. Nearly all respondents *named* robbery as being a problem.

On average, people revealed that they would get more *upset* as the intensity of a conflict increased. The regression model also shows that additional aspects of the transaction phase of the event may be important, as people reveal that they would be more upset if the other party was male. Female respondents indicated a higher degree of upset than did males. Age and household income were not related to the level of upset. Interaction effects of structural position and the potential harm doer, assessed as same sex, same age, and same socioeconomic status, do not appear to affect the level of upset. There are substantial degrees of variation in the level of upset across scenarios. We included deviation coding categories for the scenarios that indicated significantly higher levels of upset in the crime and child scenarios, and lower levels of upset in the consumer complaint situation.

Table 5.2
Regression Estimates for Pooled Models Predicting Upset, Claiming, and Aggression

	Dependent Variable					
	Upset		Claiming		Aggression	
	beta	β	beta	R	beta	R
Intercept	4.65**	—	−.80**	—	−10.20**	—
Dispute Variables						
Upset	—	—	.28**	.27	.24**	.13
Claiming	—	—	—	—	5.07**	.11
Features of Scenario						
Intensity of Conflict	.62**	.17	.18**	.05	.61**	.14
Respondent Alone	−.03	−.01	−.10	.00	−.11	.00
Sex of Harm Doer	.64**	.11	.06	.00	.30**	.04
Age of Harm Doer	−.15**	−.06	−.01	.00	.03	.02
Social Class of Harm Doer	.19**	.05	.03	.00	−.09	−.01
Attack vs. Respondent	−.24**	−.04	−.25**	−.03	−.05	.00
Respondent						
Sex of Respondent	−.90**	−.15	.66**	.11	.89**	.13
Age of Respondent	.01	.01	−.01**	−.04	−.01	−.01
Household Income	.01	.01	−.01	−.01	−.01	.00
Respondent vs. Potential Harm Doer						
Same Sex	.10	.02	.02	.00	.49**	.07
Same Age	−.03	−.01	−.16	−.02	.01	.00
Socioeconomic Status	−.11	−.02	−.02	.00	−.10	.00
Scenario (Deviation)	—	—	—	.24	—	.31
School Yard	−.49**	−.07	−.65**	−.08	.24	.00
Workplace Complaint	−.87**	−.12	−1.13**	−.07	−.27	.00
Consumer	−1.46**	−.20	−.56**	−.07	−.89**	−.04
Walking	−.98**	−.13	−.28**	−.03	.82**	.07
Crime	1.90**	.26	.07	.00	2.54**	.29
Traffic Accident	.99**	.14	.94**	.08	−1.39**	−.08
Spousal	.01	.01	−.44**	−.05	.92**	.09
Child	1.62**	.22	.70**	.06	.94**	.11
Neighbor	−.66**	−.09	−.17	−.01	−2.69**	−.07
Sporting Event	−.02	−.01	1.26**	.11	.45**	.04
Bar	.09	.01	.84**	.08	.02	.00

Notes:

R-squared (adjusted)	.18		—		—	
Model Chi-squared	—		1564.4		1575.3	
df			24		25	
Probability			p<.001		p<.001	
N	5995		5888		5888	

*p<.05   **p<.01

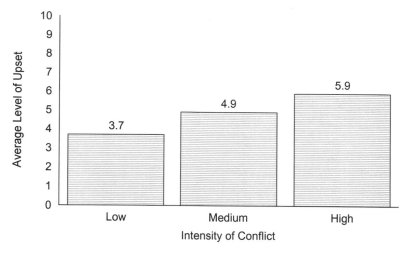

Figure 5.6
Level of Upset by Intensity of Conflict, Walking Scenario

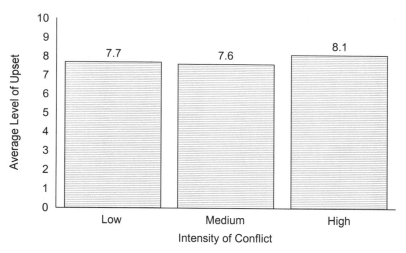

Figure 5.7
Level of Upset by Intensity of Conflict, Street Crime Scenario

Looking at claiming, as the intensity of the conflict increases, respondents, on average, admit that they would be more likely to make a claim. As with naming, there are situational differences in the likelihood of people making a claim. As shown in Figure 5.8, there is a weak relationship between the intensity of the conflict and claiming in the walking scenario.

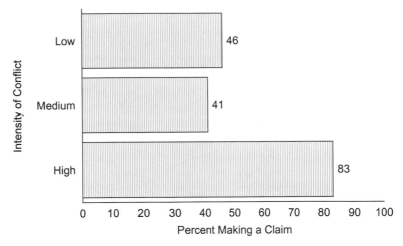

Figure 5.8
Claiming by Intensity of Conflict, Walking Scenario

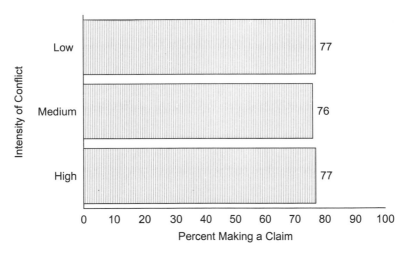

Figure 5.9
Claiming by Intensity of Conflict, Street Crime Scenario

People would more likely make a claim against the disputant in a high-intensity situation than they would in low- and medium-intensity situations. Figure 5.9, however, indicates that in a robbery many more respondents state that they would make a claim, irrespective of the intensity of the conflict.

Other factors related to claiming show that males and younger persons are more likely to make a claim. We find a moderately strong relationship between the level of upset and claiming. Respondents also indicate that they are more likely to claim if the conflict is against another person. A strength of the pooled analysis is that it enables us to identify the considerable variation in the conditions under which persons will make a claim. Respondents are more likely, than the average for all situations, to make a claim in the traffic, sporting event, and bar situations, and less likely to do so in each of the workplace situations.

There is a significant relationship between the intensity of the conflict and aggression. People say they would be more likely to use physical force against a potential harm doer in a high-intensity situation than in a low-intensity situation. This pattern is clearly evident in Figure 5.10, where more than one in three people say that they would push a person they have never before met in a street situation where they have gone to a convenience store and the person persists in calling them insulting names and pushes them (or their friend). Very few people say they would legitimate the use of aggression in a low-intensity situation where the person was yelling at them (or their friend). This situation is in marked contrast to that of robbery, shown in Figure 5.11, where over half of the respondents say they would legitimate the use of aggression, regardless of the intensity of the attack. The factorial model shows that intensity is important, but that it is not enough to explain why people would use aggression against another person.

Multivariate analysis indicates that the level of upset and making a claim are each positively related to the legitimization of aggression. Demographic factors clearly make a difference, as respondents would be more likely to use aggression if the potential harm doer is male. Males are more likely to push back than are females. Further, we find that aggression is more likely if the respondent and potential harm doer are of the same sex. The situation nonetheless has a strong effect on the use of aggression. Respondents say they are much more likely to push back in the crime scenario and far less likely to legitimate aggression if they were in a dispute with their neighbor.

An open-ended question was used to assess what people would do if the other party persisted, as we asked them if there was anything that would make them stop using physical force. This aspect is of particular interest, because it helps us understand what factors people take into consideration for the justification of the use of force and what types of things may deter violence. Looking at the results of the survey, we find that many people mention that they would reassess blame. Two examples in different domains clearly demonstrate that respondents assess whether the person is at blame. They say

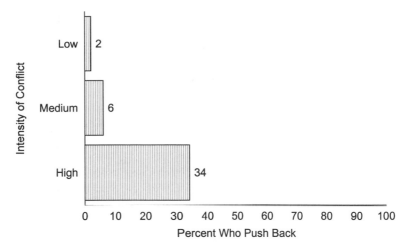

Figure 5.10
Aggression by Intensity of Conflict, Walking Scenario

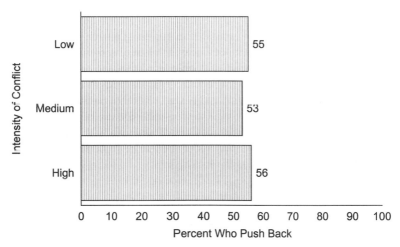

Figure 5.11
Aggression by Intensity of Conflict, Crime Scenario

If he was handicapped or drunk, I wouldn't bother, I'd just leave. (bar scenario)

If she was ill or drunk—I'd try to walk away—but definitely, I'd use physical force if I had to—to push her away and stop her from robbing us—I'd overpower her, not beat her up. (robbery scenario)

Again, at the sporting event where a person wrongfully attempts to take another person's seat, people will look to attribute blame or to excuse the person. A respondent says he would not use physical force

> . . . if the person appears mentally or physically handicapped. (sporting event)

In a street situations, one respondent points out the importance of communication before deciding whether to use force. Clearly an attribution of blame is necessary for the legitimization of aggression.

> I would reason him out. I would not use physical force if the person is smaller or can't speak English.

People also will excuse themselves of blame in some situations to legitimate the use of violence. In a robbery, for example, one woman says

> . . . if we were about equal in size I would deck her, but if we [were] not equal in size, age, etc., I would restrain and hold her for the cops.

Another, asked if anything would stop him from pushing back, said, "No, I would protect myself and my money of which I only carry very little." These are instances of self-defense in which people legitimize the use of violence.

People also say that they will come to the defense of others. We know from the helping literature (Latane and Nida 1981) that people do not always step in to help. Many of the explanations condemn the use of violence against a spouse. There are stronger condemnations of violence in the scenario where a child is being hit. Some examples about the use of force in domestic situations include statements such as the following:

> I would step between—a man never hits a lady.

> No, I don't think so (that anything will stop her from using violence). My first concern is to protect the child.

While people may feel that domestic violence is unacceptable, they also are concerned with their own safety.

> Yes, if I was the only other female in the room it would make me think twice about whether or not to use force.

There is a high degree of legitimated aggression in the leisure domain. While a majority of people say they look for assistance from bar managers, bouncers, and ticket attendants, many also indicate that their use of violence is acceptable. At a sporting event where a ticket has been paid for, respondents say they will defend their seats.

> I will defend myself if necessary. I will stand up for my rights (his ticket).

> I'd throw him down the seats, I'd beat him up for it.

It is possible to separate the respondents into a number of different social groupings (e.g., characteristics and the respondents and harm doers such as sex, age groups, socioeconomic groups, and others) or to separate particular scenarios. The factorial survey method provides much opportunity for the study of aggression that is not available using conventional data sources.

We find some clear differences in how males and females are upset and how they make claims, and in their legitimization of the use of aggression against a potential harm doer. Both males and females are more upset with male potential harm doers than female potential harm doers. Sex differences, as expected, become more pronounced when looking at aggression. Males are more likely to legitimate aggression against another male. Socioeconomic status is inversely related to the use of aggression, as is the social class of the harm doer where use of aggression is more likely to be used against a person of a lower socioeconomic group. For males and females, there is considerable variation by scenario in aggression. Notably, however, for females, the crime situation is the only scenario above the average for the proposed use of aggression. This may be due to females' far lower use of aggression compared to males.

Summary

In looking at the social construction of violence, we find that there is a high degree of tolerance for the use of violence in society. Using the Ball–Rokeach items and Dixon and Lizotte constructs, we have found a higher extent of approval for defensive than for violent use of violence in society. However, these items did not allow for an identification of whether legitimization of violence is cultural or structural.

Using a factorial survey method, we have examined a situated transaction that implies that behaviors in interpersonal conflicts are to some extent routine. This study found that there is substantial variation in the level of upset, the making of claims, and the use of aggression in each of the domains of conflict. While there is a high degree of variation across types of situations, there is evidence that individuals follow a process where they routinize their dealings with a dispute. We have found that there is variation in the naming of a dispute and in the intensity of disputes by domain. Nonetheless, on average, people tend to identify a dispute as being a potential conflict as the intensity of the conflict increases. The stark contrast between responses to violence in workplace situations versus street crime confrontations underlines the importance of situational factors in influencing the choices people make in handling conflict.

The most convincing test for situational effects in the use of physical aggression was obtained using the pooled regression models. First, this chapter has shown that the intensity of the conflict is significantly related to aggression. This is hardly surprising, since people should be expected to respond at a level of intensity consistent with that of the other party in an interaction. Second, this chapter has demonstrated that there is a low impact of difference in structural position on disputes. Difference in structural position, considered as same age, same sex, and same income, does not appear to influence whether or not respondents pursue situations as disputes. This finding is surprising, given the importance that Luckenbill and Doyle (1989) and Savitz et al. (1991) attribute to the effects of similarities and differences of combatants in predicting aggressive behavior. The exception appears when there is a similarity in gender. The fact that it does not extend beyond sex differences (to, for example, age and income) tells us the power of the generalizing effect of male on male confrontation.

Notwithstanding the null effects of most aspects of differences in structural position, this study clearly shows that demographic characteristics are quite important in understanding routine conflict. Females are more likely to be upset, whereas males are more likely to make claims and utilize aggression. The sex of the potential harm doer also is important, since males may pose a greater threat.

There may be a concern about the generalizability of these results. The response to questions about hypothetical scenarios in a survey may differ from actual behavior, because some people may never get into situations with a high intensity of conflict. Scenarios may also be artificial, in that they ask people to reveal what they would do in a particular situation rather than seeing what they actually do. We suggest that our results may be generalized, with caution, to noninterview situations. We believe that the scenarios represent a good cross section of situations of conflict in different domains. The research design of our study is appropriate, since it would be unethical to actually do many of the experimental manipulations in real life.

Returning to our original question of whether there is support for a social constructionist theory of crime and interpersonal violence, we offer the following conclusions. There is a demonstrable degree of support for approval of violence in society, but it varies by the type of situation. This finding goes against research by Berkowitz (1993) that any type of aversive stimuli causes a desire to hurt and will lead to aggression. Situational factors clearly mediate the level of violence in society. A scenario-based approach also provides limited support for Luckenbill's and Doyle's (1989) proposition that structural position is related to violence. This finding demonstrates that some aspects of structural position of potential victims and offenders may drive aggression and, ultimately, violence. We conclude that people will make choices in determining whether they would approve of the use of physical aggression in different situations. The scenario-based model presented in this chapter has shown that people will follow routines in how they evaluate whether a dispute is upsetting, whether they will make a claim, and whether they will use physical force.

Scenario-based analysis, however, may not fully reflect what people may do in real-life situations. Additional investigations are needed to understand the evolution of actual dispute situations. Empirically demonstrating the routine character of aggression and violence is an important first step to an improved understanding of these fundamental elements of aggression and violence in society. In the next chapter, we will examine crime and violence in actual disputes as we test routine conflict theory.

Chapter 6

Experience with Violence:
Routine Aspects of Conflict

Introduction

Crime and the fear of crime are important policy issues in contemporary society. Far too many persons come to experience violence either directly, as a victim of crime, or indirectly, where family or friends have suffered victimization. In this chapter, we will examine information about actual incidents of interpersonal conflict to test routine conflict theory as it draws from criminal event and interactionist theories. In chapter 3, we outlined how, theoretically, we expect that specific incidents of conflict and crime will be better understood as social rather than individual events.

Consider a traffic accident as a social event. Traffic accidents occur on an everyday basis in today's society. People often argue about who was at fault, but rarely does one party shoot the other dead, leave the scene of the accident, and later be arrested for murder. Most traffic accidents are the result of human error rather than mechanical failure, where one or both drivers erred in judgment so that a collision occurred. What would you do if you were in a traffic accident where there was "minor damage" to one or both vehicles? Would you simply take the name of the other party for insurance purposes? Would you just ask if the other person was physically okay and go about your business? Do you think you would call the police to report the accident? Or, would you, even knowing you were at least in part responsible for the accident, argue over who was *at fault*, knowing that this person would be liable for monetary damages? We saw in chapter 5 that nearly everyone is upset with the other party when they are involved in a traffic accident and that person says that they are not at fault. Suppose that the upset "victim" pulled a hand-gun from their car and proceeded to shoot and kill the other party. People's behavior in accidents can go to the extreme. Would it matter now if the gun-man was not "at fault" in the traffic accident? The police and the criminal jus-tice system will certainly be less concerned with the traffic accident than with the homicide. We may wonder how a minor traffic accident may escalate into a criminal homicide, but this incident is not an entirely unusual event, since fatal shootings over traffic accidents have occurred recently in the United States and Canada.

Throughout most of the history of criminology and criminal justice, researchers have attempted to explain crime based on the actions of offenders. Studies of how people come to be offenders, however, neglect how a victim makes contact with an offender. Routine activities theory argues that criminal acts may be better understood by taking into account the actions of offenders, victims, and guardians (Cohen and Felson 1979). Crimes are expected to be more likely to occur where there is a temporal convergence of a motivated offender, a potential victim, and a lack of a suitable guardian. A good body of evidence supports the propositions of routine activities theory about the con-vergence of lifestyle factors and crime (see Miethe, Stafford, and Long 1987; Kennedy and Forde 1990a).

The criminal event perspective differs from routine activities theories in its propositions about how actors (offenders, victims, and guardians) will make decisions in the criminal event. Hough (1987) demonstrates that offend-ers will make choices about who to victimize. Victims in crime events, it is clear, may resist their victimization (Kleck and Sales 1990). The type of guardianship also influences an offender's decision to proceed (Felson 1995). While there may be a convergence in space and time of an opportunity to offend, several factors that precede and follow a criminal event may influence whether a victimization occurs. The behavior of any one participant intersects with others as offenders, victims, and other parties who may act as guardians. We assume that routine activities theory must be expanded to look at more than motivated offenders, opportunity, or poor social conditions. The criminal event perspective assumes an integrated approach to the study of crime where the conditions that precede and follow a criminal act become important in defining the nature of crime and its participants.

Drawing from the literature on routine activities and lifestyle theories, we will identify the characteristics of offenders and victims that create opportunities for crime and victimization (Cohen and Felson 1979). This chapter will show that exposure to opportunities for violence are better understood if we consider how persons may routinely deal with conflict, that people most often will deesca-late outcomes to a resolution, but that they also will sometimes choose to esca-late conflict into violence. We will empirically demonstrate how routine conflict theory extends previous research to show factors that enhance victim risk and increase offender motivation as they are dependent upon the social context of events. We will show how routine conflict theory accounts for the actions of victims, offenders, and bystanders. Importantly, in this chapter, we will demonstrate that there is an episodic nature to events, as explained by Sacco and Kennedy (1996). We examine factors of events that may bring about the onset of conflict (precursors), the transactions themselves (crime, violence, and the use of coercion), and their aftermath (harm and consequences for action).

Precursors to Conflict

Lifestyles and Domains of Action

The precursors of a violent event may include locational and situational factors that bring people together in time and space, as argued in routine activ-

---

Box 6.1
Violence from an Event Perspective

	Characteristics of the Event	*Routine Conflict Processes Contributing to Violence*
Precursors	Location	Risky Lifestyles
	Lifestyle	
	Type of Dispute: violent or not violent	Violent Repertoires
Transaction	Who Was Involved: respondent characteristics relationship among participants number of participants	Naming or Upset
	Role of Third Parties	Making Claims and Deterring Violence
	Seriousness of Conflict	Using Violence for Compliance or Coercion
	Goals of Participants	
Aftermath	Actions of Others	Use of Police and Courts to Assign Blame and Punishment
	Harm Done	Assess Future Actions
	Resolution	Self-help or Avoidance

ities theory. To study this issue, we asked people about who was involved in their most serious incident of interpersonal conflict, where it took place, whether it happened more than one time, if violence was involved, and if they thought a crime had occurred.

Opportunities for crime are dependent upon social context. The physical location of an event might be identified as a "hot spot" for crime (Sherman, Gartin, and Buerger 1989). The physical design of a place may create a "defensible space" (Newman 1972). People also may perceive differences in the "dangerousness" of places in a city, such as a higher fear of downtown areas at night (Forde 1992). In looking at conflict, we argue that people routinize their behavior to manage risky situations. We examine the social context of interpersonal relations, domains of conflict, as it varies along several different dimensions. These include patterns of activities in physical settings, private or public character of activities, and relationships that influence the behavioral expectations of others. The social context of lifestyles has been neglected in research on lifestyle and exposure to crime (Miethe and Meier 1994).

A typology of domains and lifestyles. National crime surveys report that time and physical location are related to criminal victimization (e.g., Bureau of Justice Statistics 1992). There are differences in crime and violence by location. Sacco and Kennedy (1996) provide a framework for studying the criminal event where they designate three domains of interpersonal relations: family and household, leisure, and work. They argue that social domains may be thought of as the major spheres of life where people spend most of their time and energy. For most of us, what we do at home is different than what we do at work or what we do when we are at leisure (outside of the home). Each domain is distinguished not only by a particular location but also by a particular pattern of activity or lifestyle (Lynch 1987).

People differ in respect to the amount of time they spend in each of these domains. So, for example, for the elderly person, the social domain of the household may be of greatest importance and highest risk (see Kennedy and Silverman 1990). For younger people, little time may be spent at home because so much time is spent at work. Similarly, small children spend much of their time at home, but during the teenage years involvement in this social domain declines and involvement in the workplace and in leisure activities beyond the home increases.

Kennedy and Forde (1990a) show that personal and property crime victimization could be better explained using measures of activities in particular places (such as bars, bingo, and the theater). These measures, however, are not typically included in victimization surveys. A limited number of measures of exposure are available on the British Crime Survey, the U.S. Victim–Risk

Supplement, and the Canadian General Social Survey. We included questions about lifestyle on the current study to assess the relationship of lifestyle exposure to criminal victimization.

Sacco and Kennedy (1996) summarize how crime may develop in different domains. For example, they point out that victim surveys show that people in leisure settings who report that they frequently go out in the evening to bars also report higher rates of victimization (Sacco and Johnson 1990). Moreover, observations of barroom behavior (Stoddart 1981) and police data suggest that taverns are the site of a disproportionate amount of crime (Roncek and Pravatiner 1989). Much juvenile crime, such as drug use, vandalism, or fighting, also seems to resemble leisure pursuits (Agnew and Peterson 1989), most likely when youths are engaged in unsupervised peer activities such as "hanging out" (Kennedy and Baron 1993). Many forms of sexual assault, especially date rape, are more likely to occur in leisure environments rather than in other settings (Thompson 1986). In a similar way, homicides are most likely to occur when people are at rest, engaged in recreational pursuits in informal settings (Luckenbill 1977).

We believe that the social domain plays an important role in determining how potential outcomes for routine conflict are to be followed. We expect that disputants will pattern their behavior to conform to others' expectations depending on the social domain, and that the role of others may shift as victims or as guardians. We will present a variety of analyses to show the importance of social domains in relation to lifestyle, physical location, seriousness of the event, the use of violence, and the presence of others.

Private and public contexts of events. Important as well is the fact that these social domains differ in terms of their private or public character (Fischer 1981). The household is the most private of settings and those who we encounter there are generally well known to us. Leisure pursuits may mean more involvement with strangers or at least those we know less well. While we have tended to think of private domains as being safe and public domains as being more dangerous, this is changing. So too is the definition of privacy. The criminal event that may have occurred undetected or untreated in the "privacy" of one's home may now be likely to attract public attention and strong police action (e.g., family violence).

The identification of distinct social domains is useful in our efforts to understand differences in patterns of violent events according to interpersonal relationships. The types of people we encounter in different social domains, the relationships we have with them, and the forms of social activities that occur may affect all of the kinds of criminal events that take place, as well as the nature of our reactions to them.

Given the differing demands of each social domain, we expect to find various types of behavioral expectations that operate to influence social inter-action. These expectations are generalizable to many different situations, but they are rooted in the definition of privacy, the nature of the relationships shared with others, and the characteristics of the interaction that is to take place in these domains. What is acceptable behavior in family situations, for example, may not be allowable in work contexts. Establishing how to handle routine conflict in these situations is part of one's experience of moving through social domains, watching how others manage their relationships, and tailoring these responses to one's own needs. We can observe that the reper-toires that develop through this interaction are continuously under scrutiny. Witness the changes that have taken place in the ways in which interpersonal violence in families has been redefined and sanctioned in a way that is quite different from what was acceptable just twenty years ago.

Increasing Chances of Conflict: The Importance of Risky Lifestyles

To assess the influence of lifestyle on conflict and crime, we asked peo-ple about daytime and nighttime activities. This information provides an indi-cation of the extent to which they may be at risk for exposure to conflict and criminal victimization.

As a way of determining their daytime activities, we categorized respondents into one of the following categories: full-time work, part-time work, retired, unemployed and looking for work, and never in the labor force. We also considered types of work that may not involve remuneration, such as housework, child care, elder care, going to school, and volunteering. Each cat-egory was analyzed individually, regarding whether or not (yes or no) a per-son was involved, and as a scale where we summed up the total number of activities.

Table 6.1 provides a breakdown of the types of work and work-related activities. Approximately half of the respondents were employed full time. Nearly all people (99.8%) were involved in some kind of work or work-related daytime activity. Many said they were responsible (or shared the responsibility) for housework. On average, people were involved in 2.8 dif-ferent daytime activities. The range of involvement extends from none to seven activities, but most people reported two to four activities.

We also asked people how often in the past month they had engaged in a variety of nighttime activities. Table 6.2 shows the types of activities people may do at night and their level of participation in each. The vast majority of respondents said that they go out at night to visit friends or relatives in their own homes, to the movies or theater, to work, or shopping. Far fewer people, about one in three, said they went out to a bar at night. Very few, one in ten, said they went out to play bingo, or to gamble.

Table 6.1
Involvement in Work and Work-Related Activities

Type of Activity	N	Involved (%)
Full-time Work	1025	50
Part-time Work	413	20
Retired	336	17
Unemployed and Looking for Work	141	7
Never in Labor Force	25	1
Housework (includes shared)	1560	86
Child Care (includes shared)	686	32
Elder Care (includes shared)	316	16
Going to School	382	19
Volunteering	863	41
Total	2053	—[1]

Note: [1]Respondents may do more than one activity.

Table 6.2
Nighttime Activities of Respondents

Activity	Involved (%)	Mean Times per Month
Visit Friends or Relatives	90	4.2
Movies, Theater	83	3.4
Sports or Exercise	72	5.7
Work, Education, Volunteer at Night	68	5.1
Shop at Night	64	2.1
Bar	36	1.2
Bingo	9	0.3
Gambling	8	0.2
Any Other Activities	18	1.1

If being involved in any nighttime activity is a measure of exposure to crime, we would have to conclude that nearly everyone in society is a target for criminal victimization. Only about 3 percent of the people interviewed said they did not do any activities at night. An alternative way to look at exposure is the number of activities that people engage in over a month. Respondents averaged 4.4 types of activities in a month. Further, while people may engage in an activity, they also may vary in their level of intensity of participation. For example, the average number of times people go out to work, to school, or to volunteer at night is 5.1 times per month. Of these, many of them work five nights per week (a regular full-time night shift). Simply knowing that they are involved in the activity (full-time work) tells us as much as the number of times that they work per month (e.g., twenty times). Using a specific example, going to the bar, illustrates a similar pattern with a mean participation rate of 1.2 times per month. Most people do not go out to a bar, but those who do may report being there often (ten or twenty times per month) or even every day. To summarize these behaviors for analysis, we construct a lifestyles index that is the total of the types of nighttime activities that people were involved in over the past month.

The people in this study appear to be fairly typical of Canadians of the 1990s, with the primary emphasis on full-time work. About half of respondents are working full time but many also work part time. There are some gender differences with females, who on average are somewhat more likely to report part-time employment, housework as a task, child care, and elder care. The nighttime activities also are consistent with previous studies, such as the 1981 Canadian Urban Victimization Survey (Kennedy and Forde 1990a) and the 1989 General Social Survey (Sacco and Johnson 1990).

Lifestyle and Crime

To test the link between lifestyle and crime, we asked people whether they had been a victim of crime. An analysis of lifestyle and exposure to crime shows that people who participated in a higher number of nighttime activities were more likely to report that they had been a victim of crime. The total number of daytime activities was not related to victimization. Males and young persons were more likely to report criminal victimization. A further analysis of types of situations shows that higher victimization is reported by those who go out to a bar or out to exercise at night. Separate analyses of daytime activities indicate that higher victimization is associated with full-time work and part-time work and is lower for persons who are retired from the labor force or who have never been in the labor force. These results are consistent with our previous research (Kennedy and Forde 1990a, 1990b) on routine activities theory of criminal victimization. People's lifestyles are related to their likelihood of criminal victimization, with strong effects of demographic factors and lifestyle on the likelihood of victimization (e.g., the range extends from young males who may be employed and spending time in a bar or tavern at night to elderly persons who are retired and spend little or no time in bars at night).

While there is support for a routine activities theory of crime, we still have questions about what particular factors lead to criminal victimization and offending. Routine activities, in other words, may enhance the likelihood

Table 6.3
Location of Most Serious Conflict

Location	N	Responses (%)	Cases (%)
At Home	483	52.9	55.5
At Work	107	11.7	12.3
At School	12	1.3	1.4
In Street	39	4.3	4.5
In Bar or Restaurant	38	4.2	4.4
Park or Recreation Area	8	0.9	0.9
Elsewhere	226	24.8	25.9
Total	913	100.0	104.8

of crime, but they are not sufficient to cause it. We suggest that the routine activities of people may place them in situations where they may be at a greater risk of criminal victimization, or they may be more likely to act as offenders in the commission of crime. The routine conflict theory goes further to argue that people will have different expectations in different locations, based on routines they have learned through previous experience (resulting, in part, from their lifestyles). For example, people may engage in a "routine" in their daily lives where they may often go to bars, or they may just go to work. While these factors are associated with victimization, they are not an adequate explanation of why victimization or offending occurs. The routine aspect of a lifestyle that encourages certain ways of coping with conflict that appears in these situations is important, which will be discussed further in a moment.

Locations of Conflict

To uncover the effect of public versus private definitions of events, we asked respondents to indicate the location(s) that applied to where they had been involved in their most serious conflict. Table 6.3 clearly shows that most disputes were located in homes or in the workplace.

Based on these results, we see that a majority of interpersonal disputes occur in private settings. Knowing the location of a dispute is important, because it may influence how disputants will manage it. We know from prior studies that people define situations differently, depending on whether acts occur in private or public places (e.g., Fischer 1981). A definition of privacy influences the repertoires people will call upon to deal with a dispute. Historically, domestic violence, which most often occurs within the home, has not been defined as a criminal act by the disputants or by police. While public per-

Table 6.4
Use of Violence By Location of Most Serious Conflict

Location	Violence (Incidence)	Percent of Cases (Prevalence)
At Home	47	10
At Work	13	12
At School	2	17
In Street	12	31
In Bar or Restaurant	14	37
Park or Recreation Area	3	38
Elsewhere	44	19
Total	123	14

ceptions about privacy and violence in the home have changed, we expect that interactions will be defined as criminal violence more often if they occur in a public environment.

Table 6.4 reports the use of violence, illustrating how it differs depending on location. Respondents report that violence was used in about 14 percent of interpersonal disputes. The definition of violence was left up to the respondent, but an analysis of open-ended questions shows that most people tended to define incidents of violence as the use of some degree of physical force. Of persons involved in a conflict, there was a higher prevalence in the use of violence if they were in a public situation. This violence happens proportionately more often in bar situations, in parks, and in the street.

A different picture of violence is seen if one looks at the incidence of violence. While the prevalence of violence in disputes is lowest in the home, that is, these incidents comprised a small percentage of all violence, the incidence of violence in the home was the highest, that is, of all violent events the largest proportion occurred in the home.

The Role of Third Parties in Setting Up Routine Conflict

Third parties can be bystanders, witnesses, or participants in the development of interpersonal conflict. Victimization surveys typically provide little information on third parties beyond whether or not a third person was present at the time of the victimization (Kennedy and Forde 1990a). The paucity of information about third parties comes in part because of the many ways in which third parties may influence disputes. It is easy to operationalize the number of people involved in a dispute, but difficult to say what these people will do. We argue that the number of people in a conflict may either enhance the possibility of victimization or decrease it.

Different kinds of third parties may actually discourage crime (Felson 1995). The literature on helping behavior suggests that the behavior of others may be influenced by whether relationships between interactants are long term or short term and by gender (Eagly and Crowley 1986). Social factors may enhance a person's security if they are with or near others who may act as capable guardians. On the other hand, the literature on helping behavior also questions whether people will help another person when they are in a large group (see Latane and Nida 1981; Miller 1990). Group factors may even accelerate offending behavior, as a person may feel a need to save face where their social identity would be devalued if they did not act (Polk 1995).

The presence and type of third parties is an important variation that has been neglected in much criminological research. The contribution made by third parties can include redefining the nature of acceptable conflict, particularly as they outline for the participants the likely course of their interaction. These individuals also may provide a recount of what happened in an event. They may suggest how routine conflict strategies were followed, and they themselves learn from what they see in their own handling of future conflict. Also important in this regard is the degree of involvement of third parties in the interaction, folding into the process whereby bystanders themselves may become offenders or victims. These repertoires are learned and, as we often hear about the experiences of Good Samaritans, they are not always rewarded with thanks. Increasingly, in fact, people avoid the role of helper or intervener for fear of falling victim themselves.

Expansion of a conflict into a violent act may occur because of the role played by a third party in the dispute (e.g., a police officer), because of action by supporters who want to expand a dispute to fight on a principle, or through the actions of an audience (such as a relevant peer group who, while not a party to the dispute, may be influenced by its outcome). Disputes may expand (Mather and Yngvesson 1980–1981), where an organizational framework is imposed on the events and the relationships are encompassed by the dispute, for example, through the actions of a court in assigning guilt or innocence in attributing blame for harmful actions. It is not enough to believe that if there is someone who is large and threatening, offenders will fail to offend. Third parties can threaten, but they can cajole, embarrass, and threaten others as well. They also can promote violence through humiliation, taunting, and the like.

To assess whether people would call upon third parties for assistance in their daily lives, we asked respondents several questions about the type and extent of their social networks. People, on average, report that they talked with about five relatives per month and with about ten friends. Of those who had no contact with others, about one in five persons said they had no contact with relatives in the past month, and very few (3%) said they had no contact with friends. Regarding who they would turn to for help—friends, relatives, and formal agencies—if they had a problem, most persons said for problems at home they would most often ask for help from a friend, whereas for a large financial problem, most people report that they would go to a financial institution but many would still ask for help from a relative.

These results indicate that most of the people in the study know other people they could call upon if they had a problem. We will look at the role of third parties in conflict and what they actually do in different situations in greater detail in the next section as we examine actual transactions of conflict.

Transactions

Studying the Conflict Event

We began the questions on conflict by asking about types of conflict (see questions 17 to 46 in Appendix D). The response categories for involvement in incidents were yes or no, rather than a record of how many times for each incident. As pointed out in chapter 4, we asked respondents who had a dispute to focus on the most serious incident from the past year. If respondents identified more than one type of conflict, we asked them to indicate which conflict was the most serious. Specific questions about the most serious conflict were designed to find out who was involved, where it occurred, if it was resolved, if there were interactions with third parties, if they thought it was a crime, and the involvement, if any, of police in the dispute. Open-ended and closed-ended questions were used to obtain this information.

Females (59%) were more likely to report a conflict in the past year than were males (55%). There was a strong relation between age and involvement in a conflict in the past year. For example, young persons ages eighteen to twenty-nine were more than twice as likely to report having been in a conflict than were persons age fifty-five and over.

Number of Disputants

Disputes involved, on average, 2.6 persons, plus the respondent. Figure 6.1 shows that the most typical dispute was carried out between the respondent and only one other person (51% of the time). Third parties were involved in many instances, but this was most often with only one other person (22%). Only about 11 percent of conflicts involved five or more other persons.

Social Relationships

In most conflicts the participants were well known to each other. Table 6.5 shows that in about 90 percent of disputes between a respondent and one

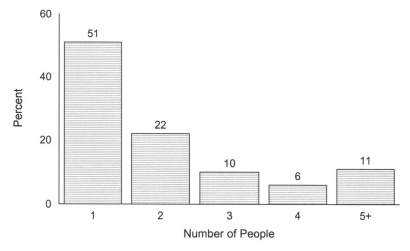

Figure 6.1
Number of People in Disputes, Not Including the Respondent

Table 6.5
Extent of Relationship between Respondent and Other Person (One Other)

Relationship	N	Respondents (%)
Well Known	349	77.0
Casual Acquaintance	41	9.0
Known by Sight	21	4.7
Did Not Know	42	9.3
Total	453	100.0

other person, these people knew each other. The number of people unknown to the respondent was higher (14%) when more than two people were involved, but the respondent was still most likely to know other people in the dispute.

We also assessed the types of social relationships between respondents and those with whom they came into conflict. Table 6.6 shows that disputes involving just one other person tended to be between a respondent and a relative (spouse, ex-spouse, or other relative). Conflicts with more than one person were less likely to have involved a spouse. For this question, people may have provided more than one answer, indicating all known relationships. We find that disputes between the respondent and a neighbor or others (e.g., a person in the workplace) are more likely to involve the respondent and two or more disputants.

Table 6.6
Relationship between the Respondent and Others
by Number of People in the Dispute

	Well Known and One disputant		More Than Two Other Disputants	
Relationship	N	(%)	N	(%)
Spouse	106	30.4	47	13.6
Ex-spouse	18	5.2	12	3.5
Other Relative	114	32.8	155	45.3
Friend	39	11.1	56	16.3
Neighbor	9	2.7	39	11.5
Other	62	17.9	138	40.3
Total	349	100.0	447	130.6

Table 6.7
Seriousness of Conflict by Location

		Other Factors in Conflict	
Location	Mean[1]	Violence (Mean)	Crime (Mean)
At Home	3.6	5.5	5.2
At Work	3.6	5.4	5.2
At School	4.4	5.4	5.9
In Street	4.0	4.8	4.5
In Bar or Restaurant	3.5	4.7	5.4
Park or Recreation Area	2.8	—[2]	—[2]
Elsewhere	3.6	4.7	4.9
All Situations	3.5	4.9	5.0

Note: [1]The scale ranged from (1), not at all serious, to (7), very serious.
[2]Too few cases to estimate.

Seriousness of a Conflict

Situational factors also may influence people's perception of the seriousness of an event. Table 6.7 shows how the seriousness of a conflict varies, depending upon location.[1] On average, conflicts are seen as neutral on a scale of "1" to "7," where "1" is not at all serious and "7" is extremely serious. If violence is involved, people tend to rate a dispute as moderately serious. Somewhat surprisingly, interpersonal violence within private settings such as the home or workplace is rated as more serious than violence in public settings such as the street or a bar. The seriousness of a conflict is again rated as higher than average if a person believes a crime has occurred. People gave equal weight to the seriousness of an event by situation if they believed a crime had occurred.

Are Conflicts "Routinized" Events?

This study has used a cross-sectional design where the single most serious incident of conflict per respondent is studied. We have shown how disputes vary in prevalence, severity, location, number of disputants, and other factors. To a great degree, though, we would like to make statements about how people learn about conflict and how they manage it.

An alternative research design would be to study people who are involved in a conflict and to see what they do in their next dispute. While we would like to know what they would do in their next dispute based on their having been involved in their current situation, we believe that a longitudinal design is impractical in that it would require a much larger sample in order to reliably identify serious types of conflict.

We believe a more reasonable solution is to draw inferences about what people would do in a subsequent situation, using information about people's lifestyles and from their responses to the hypothetical scenarios that we examined in the last chapter. Specifically, if people's routinized responses to hypothetical scenarios are consistent with what they do in actual responses, we would feel justified in saying that people's actual behavior in disputes also is a routinized behavior.

What can we conclude from this study? First, the cross-sectional results of the current chapter indicate that some kinds of everyday routine activities that people may do as part of their daily work and nighttime activities are associated with criminal victimization. It seems reasonable to expect that people who engage in a risky lifestyle will be more likely to engage in future conflicts. Second, looking at hypothetical scenarios of conflict in which we asked people about four different situations, we found that people evaluated the situational dynamics of each situation. Those people who stated that they would use aggression in one situation would not necessarily use it in all situations. The intensity of the dispute was related to the use of violence. The location of the dispute influenced the outcome, as did some aspects of the structural position of the participants (e.g., male-on-male confrontation). Importantly, the hypothetical scenarios demonstrated that people will look to the situational dynamics of a situation to call upon a repertoire of responses, even in situations where they may not have previously experienced the type of dispute. This study clearly has shown that in situations of high intensity and where there was an approval of violence, people would routinize the use of aggression across these scenarios, and that where there was a disapproval of violence, people would not use it across situations.

Given these results, we believe it is valid to say that people apply what they say to what they do. This is not a statistical inference when we compare the results of hypothetical conflicts to actual conflicts. We are looking at patterns within different sets of results. We believe that it is valid to draw parallels between the hypothetical scenarios and actual behavior: for example, intensity of hypothetical conflict and seriousness of actual conflict; sex of aggressor versus sex of disputant; domain of hypothetical conflict versus actual location of conflict; hypothetical scenario versus actual type of conflict; who they would call upon versus who they did call upon for assistance, and so on. The results of this study provide strong support for the argument that conflict is routinized because of the similarities in what people said in the hypothetical scenarios and in what they actually did.

The process of routinization of conflict involves decision making within disputes. People are able to call upon a repertoire of conflict experiences so they may deal with conflicts ranging from trivial disputes to serious crimes. People will make choices in situations of conflict to direct the outcome of a dispute. Some of these choices will resolve disputes and others will lead people into criminal offense. We will illustrate the consistency in dealing with disputes using responses from open-ended questions to show how people actually used, or suffered from, some sort of coercive action in their most serious dispute.

Coercion

Tedeschi and Felson (1994) suggest that the basic elements of decision-making processes in conflict can be understood through a study of coercive acts defined as ". . . taken with the intention of imposing harm on another person or forcing compliance." Coercive actions may come as threats, bodily force, and punishment.

Threats

A threat is a communication that a person intends to harm another person. Tedeschi and Felson (1994, 169–70) define two forms of threats where one is contingent and the other is noncontingent. In a contingent threat, a person will place a demand for compliance. In a noncontingent threat, a person simply says he or she will harm the target person. Tedeschi and Felson (1994, 170) also state that threats may often be tacit, implied, or nonspecific.

As we described in chapter 4, when we looked at general experiences with conflict, we asked people to describe what happened and why the act they chose was the most serious. This question was not designed to specifically identify the use of threats. It also may not have allowed an identification of the use of nonverbal communication amongst disputants. It is not possible to identify the extent of the time that threats were used because of the sample size and because the question was not designed to ask about specific aspects of threats. We can only conclude that threats are evident in all domains of conflict. Nonetheless, we did find a large number of clear examples of threats in our study of social conflict. Rather than using scales designed to test the strength of people's responses to these threat situations, we left our questions open ended. This provided us with a more qualitative view of how people define and respond to threats and punishments. These descriptions form the bases for the evidence provided here concerning the use of coercion in disputes. We find that threats were used in all situations including, for example, crime events, arguments over money, family-based conflicts, and others.

Contingent threats were evident in all social domains. For example, in a crime act, where a person was robbed, the respondent says that a "University age young man robbed him and threatened him with assault." This threat can be seen as contingent, because the target person was threatened with harm if he did not turn his property over to the robber. Another contingent threat appeared in an argument over money. A respondent finds herself in a situation where her ex-husband threatened nonpayment of child support if the mechanisms for payment were not changed. She

> asked him to pay child support and asked him to pay for snowpants. He said, "Only if maintenance enforcement program was used" so he could claim payments on (his) income tax.

He placed his parental obligations as contingent on her going along with changes in how payments were made, so he would receive a tax benefit. Several other respondents indicated threats over financial matters where child support was involved.

Some threats may not have been carried out. For example, a landlord and tenant dispute involved noise from a tenant. A person came home and was greeted by friends. It turned out to be a noisy greeting. A neighbor subsequently complained to the landlord. The respondent to the survey says that his landlord said, "Be quiet or we'll kick you out."

The respondent noted this as a conflict but at the same time he did not see it as being a very serious matter. We do not know if the landlord would actually have done this, or if it would have taken multiple incidents for an eviction to occur. Nonetheless, the threat was issued as a demand that the residents of the apartment modify their behavior if they wished to continue living in the unit.

There were a variety of incidents involving neighbors. Some of these were cited as serious threats. For example, a noncontingent threat was described in a neighborhood dispute where the "neighbor threatened to poison my cat." In another argument between neighbors over a property line, a contingent threat was issued to get off of the property or violence would ensue. The respondent describes it as

> He claimed I was standing on his property and he said he was going to "move" me. I said, "O.K., let's go," but he did not budge. He was a chicken.

The respondent clearly interprets the outcome of this event as one where he humiliated the other person by calling his bluff.

Looking at family disputes, we found several incidents that involved contingent threats. For example, a respondent was told that his relationship with his wife would end if he did not modify his behavior, as

> she wanted him to drink less and spend more time getting involved with her kids and their outings.

This example and many other family disputes were described as moderately serious events. Some others involving noncontingent threats clearly were more serious. A respondent says that

> It is pretty bad when you are afraid to go out after dark because of your mother-in-law and sister-in-law. We moved to get away from them, but they saw us and followed us home so now they know where we live. My father-in-law doesn't get involved at all.

The respondent clearly interpreted the stalking on the part of her in-laws as an implied threat. She expresses "fear" of her in-laws based on possible future interactions.

In workplace disputes, we find several incidents where the tables are turned on potential offenders through use of contingent threats. For example, one respondent describes his situation in the following way:

> Three guys were fired. They were a little upset so that they came with a baseball bat, a tire iron, and a knife. They made death threats. So, I was not going to fight them. I wanted to change their minds and not hurt them. So I pulled a gun and shot between their feet and left holes in the pavement in Dallas.

The respondent saw the situation as being one where the use of a gun was justified. Would he have actually shot the "offenders" if they continued? The threat appears to have been enough to resolve the incident from the point of view of the respondent. The potential offenders also withdrew from the situation. There are other ways to resolve disputes other than potentially violent gunfire. Consider the situation where a potential offender came into the workplace and made a crime threat. A respondent describes the situation in the following way:

> A tax payer, frustrated with taxes on several business properties and economic problems, threatened to shoot me. I said "Hello" and he took it downhill from there. It may not be serious but you'll never know.

What was it about this situation that it was resolved without the use of violence from either party? Was this person better prepared to deal with conflict so it was defused?

Overall, we have found evidence that threats, contingent and non-contingent, appear in all domains of social conflict. Threats varied in intensity from trivial to very serious. We cannot estimate whether threats lead to a greater number of resolutions of conflict, nor whether threats lead to resolution of few conflicts. We do find, though, that threats act to direct social conflict. Of the disputes where we were able to identify decision-making processes in a dispute, threats were more commonly used than were physical force and punishment.

Physical Force

Tedeschi and Felson (1994, 168) define bodily force as "the use of physical contact to compel or constrain the behaviors of another person." We find many examples in our study of social conflict where physical contact was made between disputants. However, respondents gave stronger descriptions of the extent of the violence against the person rather than the intent of the person in their use of violence.

Many of the respondents who were involved in a crime act (robbery or assault), either on the street or at work, reported that physical force was used. For example, a respondent says that there was a

> shoplifter in my store. I phoned the police. He struggled and pulled out a knife and fled. The police came soon after and arrested him.

The physical force was used in the attempt to get away. Several other respondents indicated that they had used physical force in robberies where they hit or attempted to hit offenders who were successful in robbing them. The objective of their use of force was to stop the robbery or assault, though they were unsuccessful. The results of this survey are consistent with National Crime Surveys, which suggest that use of physical force to stop a robbery meets with limited success. It is more likely that a person who fights back in a robbery will be more severely hurt than someone who does not (see analyses of the National Crime Survey).

Bodily force also may be used in family disputes. We identified a number of instances where males used physical force against women. A respondent describes a dispute over where she should live. She says that she

> would not go back to her boyfriend and she was subsequently grabbed and slapped.

Physical force is used in this instance as the offender tries to coerce her to go along with him. Physical force also can be perpetrated by men against men in family based disputes. One case involves a fight between a boyfriend and an ex-spouse. The fight is described by the ex-wife, who says, "It was to do with my ex-husband visiting the children."

The ex-husband's use of physical force was intended to coerce the ex-wife and boyfriend to accept his rights to visit the children. However, instead of a resolution, the respondent described this as an ongoing and unresolved dispute.

Research shows that most domestic violence is perpetrated by men but that women may be involved (Gelles and Straus 1988). We identified several incidents in this study that involved women using physical force. For example, a respondent was involved in a dispute because she was evicting her sister-in-law from her residence. She tells us that

> the day I kicked my sister-in-law out, her mother barricaded me in my kitchen and they both kept punching me in the face.

The bodily force was used in an attempt to force compliance on her staying in the kitchen. The women also were attempting to force her to change her mind on where the sister-in-law was to live. It turns out that the sister-in-law was successfully evicted from the house. Nonetheless, force was used in an attempt to coerce compliance.

Punishment

Tedeschi and Felson (1994, 171) define "punishment as an action performed with the intention of imposing harm on another person." Harm may be physical, involving a deprivation of resources, or it may be social, involving harm to the identity of the person as a lessening of his or her power or status.

We find a variety of examples in our study of social conflict that clearly meet Tedeschi's and Felson's criteria for punishment as a coercive action. Most of these events were conflicts where the person did much more than was necessary to obtain compliance from the other party in the conflict. This survey found examples of punishment in all domains of conflict. Following are some examples that illustrate how punishment is used in attempts to direct the outcome of events.

In a crime event, a person was charged with assault where he says he was being victimized in an attempted robbery with a knife. The respondent's ear had been cut in half. He says,

> I went crazy to defend myself and beat him severely. I was charged with criminal assault for using excessive force in defending myself.

The use of bodily force was an act of self-defense in this situation, but the extent of the physical force exceeded that allowed by law to defend himself. The respondent acted to stop any further harm against himself from the potential offender, but the severe beating can be interpreted as a punishment of the offender.

This study of the general population identified only a small number of people who were involved in actual crime events (robbery and assaults). We did ask a similar question in the hypothetical scenarios about crime. We asked people what would stop them from pushing back against the offender. Some people simply said nothing would stop them from pushing back, as he deserved it. Others described how they would hurt the offender. These responses are clearly punitive, as they go beyond what it would take for the person to get away from the crime event.

Punishments need not be physical. Several respondents described how they were punished monetarily in landlord–tenant disputes. Consider the situation where a landlord punishes a tenant for failure to clean an apartment when vacating. The tenant describes the situation as follows:

> Late notice was given. The landlord said if the apartment was cleaned that the damage deposit would be returned. We cleaned the apartment and moved out. The landlord said the inside of the stove had to be cleaned and then the damage deposit would be returned. The stove wasn't cleaned. The landlord then insisted late notice was given.

The respondent did not continue with the dispute, and the deposit was forfeited for noncompliance in the cleaning of the suite.

In another neighborhood dispute a respondent describes an incident where a person was upset about people parking in front of his house. The respondent says,

> He was putting a note on my shield so I went to see what the problem was. I read it and told him the street was a public area, and he could not ban people from parking in front of his house. He said, "There will be consequences if this continues," but he didn't say what. Neighbors told me he has scratched their vehicles with a key or put toothpicks in their door locks to prevent keys from working. Some of my employees have had notes put on their vehicles when they come to my house and park in front of his house.

This person's actions appear to be directed as acts of punishment against people who park in front of his house. They are physical acts, but they are acts against the property of people with whom he is in dispute over parking in front of his house.

Several acts of punishment were reported in family based conflicts. For example, in a child custody dispute, a respondent says that he is involved in

> an ongoing (dispute over) access to contact with his son. It's parental alienation using legal tactics in a court dispute over access to my son.

Restricting access to his child is being used as a punishment for noncompliance in other areas of the divorce settlement. In another child custody case, a mother did not have the father's name placed on the birth certificate. He says,

> She didn't want me to see my son. Her parents said my name was not on the birth certificate, so I had no right to access.

This situation is coercive in that it is meant to challenge both his identity as a father and to deprive him of access to his son. Whether or not there are justifications for this situation, the act is one that is directed as a punishment against him. In both of these incidents, the respondents make statements that suggest that they do not believe that the legal system would help them. Acts of punishment are used against the respondent to direct the ongoing disputes.

> Physical force was reported in an ongoing domestic argument where my ex-spouse sexually assaulted me. The other time he just threatened to do it.

Physical force is clearly coercive, as the woman was physically forced into sexual relations when she did not want involvement with her ex-spouse. The forced sexual relations in this act are a punishment for failure to conform to his earlier demands.

The earlier examples of coercion in family situations involved situations where a divorce, separation, or breakup had occurred. Punishment also may be used in intact family units. This survey found many instances of conflict in families, some of which involved physical force.

Family situations involving punishment need not involve physical force. This act is compatible with research on psychological abuse (Gelles and Straus 1985). For example, a woman describes a conflict with her spouse over her work-situation in the following way:

> Because I don't work, he feels hard done by. He always opposes my views.

She describes challenges to her social identity in public situations that act to humiliate her so that she will change her views on her work.

Aftermath of Conflict

In considering the aftermath of a transaction, we are interested in the degree that an individual has been harmed and in the resources needed to aid in his or her recovery. We can look to see who people may call to assist them in dealing with conflict and crime. Will they resolve the conflict? What brings people in a dispute to call upon third parties? When will disputes be resolved, and how do victims of crime deal with it?

Substantive tests of victimization theories and research on the aftermath of criminal events have been limited because of the type of information collected in the national crime surveys. Studies of victims in clinical studies suggest that the crime and conflict can have long-term, debilitating effects, such as post–traumatic stress disorder. Quite clearly, one important aspect of predatory crime is the victim and offender relationship. There is an assumption in the victimization literature that this factor may deter the reporting of a crime, particularly if the problem involves family members who have an ongoing and intimate relationship. By the same logic, the more distant the relationship between the parties, the more likely that one of them will call the police to deal with the problem (Kennedy 1988). What, however, is the role of third parties? Victimization surveys have identified that people will call the police in about one-half of incidents. National crime surveys, by design, have focused on a formal response to crime to address why people will or will not

Table 6.8
Principal Person Who Intervened in Conflict,
by All Persons and Involvement in Conflict

Who Intervened? (Relationship to Respondent)	N	All Respondents (%)	Conflict (%)
Police	67	3.3	21.8
Family Member	51	2.5	16.7
Friend	43	2.1	14.0
Lawyer	31	1.5	9.9
Neighbor	12	0.6	3.8
Social Worker	9	0.4	2.9
Stranger	4	0.2	1.3
Other	91	4.4	29.4
Total (Involved in Conflict)	308	—	100.0
Total	2,042	100.0	

call the police. This study looks at whether third parties were involved in interpersonal conflicts and how their involvement may have influenced the process of disputes to resolution or escalation.

Looking at interpersonal conflict, we told respondents that, "Sometimes other parties intervene in conflicts, for example, friends, neighbors, police, lawyers, or others. " We asked if anyone intervened and, if so, who principally intervened in their conflict. We did not provide a list of persons, instead asking people to indicate the identity of the person. We found that someone intervened in about one in three conflicts (37%). Correlational analysis indicates that there is a weak relationship between the number of people involved in a dispute and the likelihood of an intervention.

Table 6.8 provides a breakdown of principal persons who intervened in a conflict as a percentage of the sample and as a percentage of all conflicts. We estimate that about 4 percent of all adults in Manitoba and Alberta called the police to intervene in a dispute in the past year. Of all possible third parties that people could call, police were the most common one called to intervene in a conflict, contacted in about one in four disputes. A significant number of people indicated other formal responses to conflict where they called either a lawyer or social worker. Many interpersonal conflicts, as we would expect, are dealt with informally by family members, friends, neighbors, and sometimes strangers. Other types of third parties very often included coworkers, supervisors, and managers.

The seriousness of the event is related to whether a third party is called upon to intervene in a situation. This relationship can be seen by looking at per-

Table 6.9
Calls to Third Parties by Location of Conflict, Sex of Respondent

Location and Sex	N	Calls (%)
Males		
At Home	67	30
At Work	33	44
At School	—	—[1]
In Street	9	45
In Bar or Restaurant	8	35
Park or Recreation Area	—	—[1]
Elsewhere	33	33
All Situations (males)	148	34
Females		
At Home	90	34
At Work	22	65
At School	6	69
In Street	8	50
In Bar or Restaurant	7	58
Park or Recreation Area	—	—[1]
Elsewhere	45	45
All Situations (females)	162	39
Total (both)	310	36

Note: [1]Too few cases to estimate.

ceptions of seriousness of conflict where there is a moderately strong correlation between seriousness of conflict and whether a third party intervened in the conflict. The relationship also is indicated by the likelihood of a third-party intervention, the use of violence in the conflict and people's perceptions of whether the conflict was a crime. We find that the likelihood of a third-party intervention is nearly twice as high, on average, if violence is used in a dispute. Interventions took place in 61 percent of disputes where violence was involved and in 33 percent of disputes where violence was not involved. A similar pattern is found in disputes where people think that a crime has occurred, when someone intervened in 61 percent of disputes where people think a crime may have occurred, and in 29 percent of disputes where people do not think a crime was involved.

Why is it in some situations where violence occurred and crimes may have occurred that people did not call upon a third party? To consider this we have to take into account the social domain where the interaction occurred. Table 6.9 provides a breakdown of the percentage of interventions by third

Table 6.10
Calls to Third Parties by Location of Conflict, by Violence and Crime

Location	Violence		Crime	
	N	(%)	N	(%)
At Home	28	63	56	63
At Work	10	75	28	73
At School	—	—¹	—	—¹
In Street	6	67	9	58
In Bar or Restaurant	7	56	6	66
Park or Recreation Area	—	—¹	—	—¹
Elsewhere	22	52	27	52
All Situations	71	62	116	62

Note: ¹Too few cases to estimate.

parties by location for the total sample and by sex of the respondent. It shows that the prevalence of calls to third parties is lowest when a conflict occurs within the home, where most conflicts occur. People consider many of these events to be of low seriousness. This is consistent with research on family violence, which shows people believe that actions in the home are a private matter not to be discussed with other people, or reported to the police. The prevalence of calls to third parties is highest when a conflict occurs at work.

An analysis of calls that take into account the gender of the respondent shows that males and females are about equally likely to call upon a third party across all of the situations. This pattern holds true for conflicts in the home, but differences emerge for conflicts in the workplace and in a bar or restaurant. Females were more likely than males to report that they called upon a third party in these situations. While a home situation and a work situation may both be private domains, a workplace and a bar or restaurant share the likelihood that a manager, supervisor, or coworker may be called upon as potential guardians. At the same time, similar to conflicts in the home where an expected guardian becomes a criminal offender, conflicts in the workplace can be between supervisors and employees or with coworkers. A testament to this is the fact that workplace violence is a leading cause of injury in the United States and Canada.

The likelihood of a call to a third party increases as the seriousness of a conflict increases. Calls to a third party are about two times as likely if a conflict involves violence and occurs in the home. The prevalence of calls is about 1.5 times as likely on average if violence is involved in all other situations (Table 6.10). A similar pattern in calls to third parties is evident if people consider the conflict a crime.

Additional analysis of calls to third parties shows that the type of person who may be called upon differs by situation and by the respondent's perception of the event. The reliability of estimates, when using several variables in a crosstabulation analysis, is such that we can identify some broad-based patterns in relationships, but we cannot state precise percentages for all categories of locations. There are too few cases of people involved in conflicts in school settings and park or recreation areas. Despite a relatively large sample size, we can only discuss conflicts in the home, workplace, and street, and in some leisure settings.

The results of the study suggest that if conflict occurs in the home and a crime is perceived, the police are the party most likely to be called. If the action is not perceived as a crime, the most likely third party called is another family member. Incidents in a workplace situation follow a similar pattern with calls to police when a crime is perceived, but with calls to a manager or coworker when a crime is not evident. Incidents in a leisure setting, such as a bar or restaurant, are far less likely to involve intervention from the police. People rely on others such as bouncers and bartenders or their friends to deal with these incidents, whether or not they perceive the event as a crime. Respondents indicate that they rely predominantly on the police if a conflict occurs in the street and they see it as a crime. Informal third parties, such as family and friends, were called upon during conflicts for events not perceived as crimes.

Resolution

Approximately 65 percent of all interpersonal conflicts are resolved. Males and females are equally likely to resolve a conflict. Younger persons are less likely than older persons to resolve a dispute. Total household income was not related to whether a dispute was resolved. We asked respondents involved in a conflict who started it. Figure 6.2 shows that a conflict is much more likely to be resolved if the respondent started it than if the other person or a third party initiated it.

The likelihood of resolution lessens as the seriousness of the conflict increases. Figure 6.3 illustrates that fewer disputes will be resolved if violence is involved, or if a crime is perceived. The lower prevalence of resolution can be explained in part by the seriousness of the conflict, since conflicts involving violence or a perceived crime also are those incidents that tend to be seen as being more serious events.

The location of an event also can influence whether or not it will be resolved. Persons were most likely to report a resolution if the event occurred in a workplace setting (75%) and least likely to report resolution if it occurred in a bar or recreational setting (58%). A relatively high number of incidents in street settings (69%) were reported as being resolved. Street incidents, how-

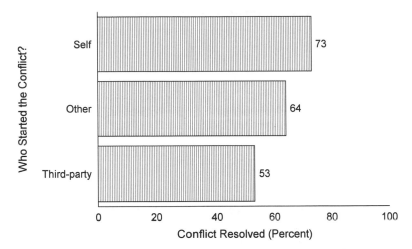

Figure 6.2
The Conflict was Resolved by Who Started the Conflict

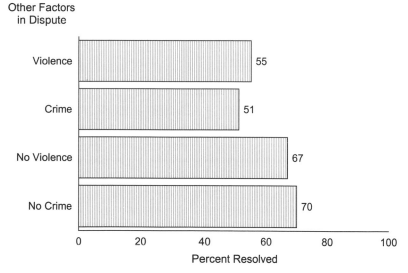

Figure 6.3
The Dispute was Resolved by Whether There Was Violence or Crime

ever, did not always involve a crime. Most instances of conflict in the home also were resolved (65%).

When third-party interventions occurred, they most often lead to a resolution of a dispute (51%). Third-party interventions, however, did not change the situation in many (37%) conflicts, and even made things worse in some cases (12%). Third-party interventions leading to a resolution appear to have been most successful when done in a workplace setting (59% better; 16% worse), and least successful when carried out in a bar setting (37% better; 28% worse). Males and females were equally likely to report a resolution if a third party was involved. There were no differences in the success of third-party interventions by the age of the respondent, nor by household income.

Going it Alone

We know from victimization surveys that a large number of people choose not to report crimes to the police (see McClintock 1970; Sacco and Johnson 1990). It has been argued in the victimology literature that this underreporting reflects the inadequacies of the formal criminal justice system to protect people from crime. Kennedy (1988) suggests that people may go it alone to resolve crimes. The victimology literature has neglected the possibility that people may seek resolution of crime and conflict on their own.

A large number of people (64%) either chose not to call upon a third party or a third party was unavailable to intervene in the conflict. Looking at all instances of conflict, people report a higher rate of resolution if a third party is not involved (71%) than if they intervened (57% resolved) in the conflict. These results, of course, reflect the fact that the resolution of conflict will be higher in less serious incidents where third parties are neither desired nor present. Looking specifically at resolution and whether police were called to intervene, we find a similar pattern. Resolution of the dispute is lower if the police are called (52%) than when they are not (68%).

Additional analysis, taking into account whether people think a crime occurred, helps differentiate when people will go it alone. Figure 6.4 shows that rates of resolution are significantly lower when people think a crime has occurred. Calling a third party or going it alone yields about equal rates of resolution when a crime is perceived. However, going it alone rather than calling a third party will yield resolution of a dispute about 8 percent more often.

A similar pattern in the resolution of conflicts is found when calls to the police are examined for disputes that were perceived as crimes. People say the dispute was resolved about one-half of the time when they felt the incident was a crime. Figure 6.5 shows that resolution does not depend on making a call to the police when the incident is perceived as a crime. About half of these incidents were resolved. Resolution of the dispute is substantially higher, as we would expect, if people did not feel a crime was involved and they did not call the police.

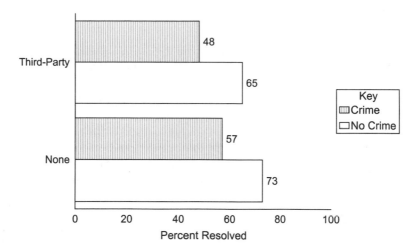

Figure 6.4
Resolution of Conflict and Involvement of
Third Parties by Whether the Dispute Was a Crime

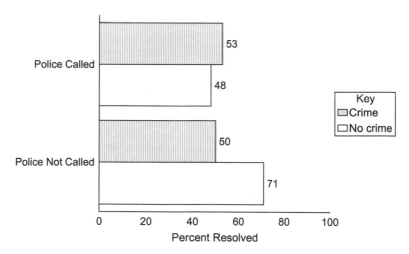

Figure 6.5
Resolution of Conflict When Police are Called, by Crime

These results indicate that a large number of disputes may be resolved informally, where a person may attempt to solve it on his or her own. Women are somewhat more likely to use the police to assist in a dispute if it is a crime or crime attack. The lower rate of resolution when the police are involved also reflects a lower rate of resolution for more serious and ongoing disputes.

Summary

This study has examined how people deal with experiences of conflict in their everyday lives. We found a clear relationship between people's risky lifestyles with both crime and conflict. These findings were generally consistent with previous research on routine activities theory, as risky lifestyles have been shown to lead to a greater likelihood of criminal victimization. This chapter also has examined factors such as the location of the event, the victim and offender relationship, the role of third parties, and others. Results have shown that most conflicts are not considered serious, but that conflicts can be used as methods to coerce others. Support was evident for routine conflict theory in reports of episodic variations in conflict and criminal victimization.

In using a social survey, we were able to draw upon information that is both consistent with and extends upon that from victimization surveys. These results have demonstrated that people will act differently to conflict, depending upon situational factors. Overall, these results show that most persons encounter conflict in private situations. Few cases of conflict involved crime or violence. People far more often were able to solve instances of conflict, even for events they rated very serious. These results have indicated that most people share a common repertoire for dealing with conflict. Conflict is routinized, so people faced with severe or minor disputes will use common strategies to defuse and deescalate conflict. The results of our study of experiences with conflict were consistent with people's attitudes toward conflict. Recall from chapter 5 that we asked all people what they would do if they were involved in different types of hypothetical disputes. This chapter demonstrated that reported acts of conflict were consistent with what people said they would do. We suggest that people are able to draw from experiences of trivial conflicts, routinizing their experiences with conflict, so that most people are better able to deal with social conflict ranging from trivial incidents to criminal victimization.

Considering coercion in disputes, where a person may use conflict to direct another person's behavior, this chapter has presented evidence in support of interactionist theory that people use coercion to direct another's behavior—through threats, physical force, and punishment. While we were not able to identify the prevalence of the use of coercion, we nonetheless found clear statements from respondents where coercion was used to direct the outcomes of disputes.

This chapter has provided a basic test of the coincidence of routine conflict and crime. The study has limited the analysis of interpersonal conflict to explanations of only the most serious conflict that happened in the past year. While we would have liked to test how individual people dealt with specific and different types of conflict, we were ethically bound to study only what they reported. We have confidence in the validity of these results, because there are many consistencies in respondents' strategies for dealing with the experiences of conflict and people's reports on how they would deal with hypothetical conflict (chapter 5). A further method to test it is to go to a group where conflict and crime often occur to see what they do to resolve it. We proceed, in the next chapter, to test the theory of routine conflict in a study of street youths and violence.

Chapter 7

⊂⊰◈⊱⊃

Street Youth and Violence

Stephen Baron, University of Windsor[1]

Introduction

In the last two chapters, Kennedy and Forde have examined how conflict emerges and evolves utilizing information from a survey of a general population. This chapter presents the results of a field study of conflict in a sample of homeless street youths. The application of a theory of routine conflict is explored in a test of the generalizability of conflict styles in a general population to a group with a high rate of violent offending (see Baron 1995). A field study also provides an opportunity to uncover possible differences in conflict management styles that may exist between these two types of populations.

Street Youth

Street youth as a term has rarely been well defined, but usually it refers to youth who have run away, been expelled from their homes, and/or who spend some or all of their time in various public locations. Past research suggests a heterogeneity in street lifestyle and street youth as a group. The street population is made up of both youth who "hang out" on the street on a regular and permanent basis and youth whose street life participation is more sporadic. It contains those who attend school and those who have dropped out. Some live at home, others are on their own, and others are on the street. Some work full time or part time, others rely on state assistance, social agencies, or crime to support themselves. Some of these youth are preteens, others are in their mid-twenties. Thus, involvement in street life is better characterized as a continuum of involvement with a high degree of heterogeneity in street life than as a categorical entity where a youth is or is not on the street.

Field Methods

For this study, 125 male respondents were interviewed in a field setting, with sampling based on the following criteria:

- participants must be male
- they must be age twenty-four and under
- they must have left or finished school
- they must spend at least three hours a day, three days a week, "hanging around" on the street or in a mall.

The rationales for these criteria were (1) to avoid potential ethical problems of a male researcher inquiring about intimate areas of female respondents' lives[2] (sexual abuse, sexual assault, and prostitution); (2) to cover the age range of those described as street youth (Caputo and Ryan 1991, 8–10); (3) to eliminate those who were not candidates for full-time employment; and (4) to obtain a sample of "serious" or "at risk" youth while avoiding the "weekend warriors." Although the fourth criterion left the door open for the inclusion of respondents who were employed, lived at home, and spent minimal time on the street, the data show that the average respondent was essentially on the street full time, having made it home for about four months in the prior year.

The data collection was completed over a three-month period, from May to July 1995 in Edmonton, Alberta, one city included in the general survey described earlier. The study took place in and around the downtown business core of the city, which is bordered by the local skid row and "inner city." The area contains a mix of commercial and financial establishments surrounded by bars, pawnshops, hotels, shelters, detoxification centers, rooming houses, rundown residential units, and abandoned buildings.

Sample selection began with the interviewer situating himself in geographical areas known to be frequented by street youth. Potential respondents were approached, alerted to the project, and screened for study eligibility. Contacts with some additional respondents were initiated by youths who had learned of the researcher's presence and had solicited interviews, or through introductions from previously interviewed youths.

Those youth meeting the selection criteria were then provided with more information on the study and were asked to participate.[3] After granting consent, the youth were taken to be interviewed in the comfortable and sheltered conditions of one of the food courts that dot the many malls in the down-town core. These interviews averaged an hour and ten minutes in length. Upon completion of the interview, the respondents were awarded twenty dollars in food coupons, which could be redeemed at a popular fast food restaurant.

The researcher began and ended each day by returning to the locations where he had come into contact with previous respondents. This allowed him to follow up on the youths' situations and observe and gather more information on their behaviors, which he recorded in field notes at the end of each day. This process also filled periods of down time where there were no new people to be approached or found.

Looking at characteristics of the sample, all of these street youth were male. Their average age was about nineteen ($\overline{x}$ = 18.8). All but four of these youths had spent some time during the year living away from their parents, and all but eight had no fixed address during the last year (N = 117). Their average amount of time spent homeless in the previous year was about five months ($\overline{x}$ = 5.3). Their level of education is below what would be expected for their age, averaging just over a grade nine education ($\overline{x}$ = 9.6), with an average legal income of just under $3,000 a year.

Having looked at routine conflict in a more general population, we will move now to replicate much of the earlier analysis utilizing this sample of street youths, exploring the similarities and differences between this "at risk" group and the more general population. We begin this examination by returning to the issue of interpersonal conflict and asking our street youths about the forms of conflict that were reviewed in chapter 4.

Street Youth Versus a General Population

Experiences with Conflict

Consistent with the analysis in chapter 4, we asked these youths if they had experienced any of the seven types of conflict outlined earlier (crime attack, threat of crime attack, argument over money, argument with landlord, argument with neighbor, conflict with family, any other conflict). When we asked street youths to report their involvement in these different types of conflicts, all but one (99%) reported being involved in some type of conflict during the prior year. Their near universal involvement in conflict far surpasses the 43 percent level reported by the general population. This immediately suggests that street youths are much more likely to find themselves in a conflict than are actors leading more conventional lifestyles. A demonstration of the extent of street youth conflict is the discovery that almost half of the street respondents indicated that they had been involved in a crime attack in the last year (48%). This number dwarfs the 3.6 percent reported by the conventional sample. Similarly, close to two-thirds (63%) of the street youths sampled were involved in some type of threatened crime attack. This compares to the 6.6 percent found in the conventional sample. However, the most common type of conflict (75%) within the street youth sample involved arguments over money. All of these results suggest that in comparison to a conventional sample, the street sample is more likely to have experienced conflicts, and street youth are at a greater risk to find themselves in criminal-type conflicts.

Legitimization of Violence

Chapter 5 discusses how the use and approval of violence may differ between segments of the population. There are some suggestions that certain populations legitimate the use of violence more than others. Much of the general population clearly legitimates the use of violence under certain circumstances. Is it possible that support for violence is even greater in other segments of society? One population that comes to mind when speaking of support for violence, subcultures of violence, or violent participation is street youth.

The review of the support or legitimization for violence in chapter 5 has revealed that the general population is supportive of violence under certain conditions. Comparing the responses of the street youth in this study with those results obtained from the general population, we discover a number of similarities. First, like the general population, most street youths would approve of a police officer striking an adult male attempting to flee custody (59% vs. 67%) or of attacking the officer with his fists (92% vs. 88%). Thus, street youths, like the general population, view police force as being legitimate in certain circumstances. However, compared to the general population, street youths are much more likely to legitimate the use of violence in other situations, including where an adult hits a child (77% vs. 26%), where a male stranger is striking a female (92% vs. 56%), or where their dwellings have been broken into (82% vs. 47%). These three measures together indicate a greater support for a defensive use for violence in the street youth than what is found for a general population. There is near universal support for the use of violence in these situations by street youth, with a full 94 percent of the respondents indicating an approval for violence in at least two out of these three situations. This approval of defensive violence is much higher than the two-thirds of conventional respondents, who would favor defensive use of violence. Similarly, we discover that the street youth score much higher on the violent attitude items. Forty-two percent of the street sample indicated that they would approve of the use of violence in at least one of the four violent attitude items (protest march, drunk bump, obscene language, and murder suspect). This is considerably higher than the 25 percent found in the more conventional sample. What this suggests is that street youths' support for violence is high in situations where there is a general public support for violence, but they also condone violence under circumstances where there is ambiguity toward, or disapproval of, violence from the general public.

Approval of Violence and Crime

The subculture of violence thesis predicts a relationship between approval of violence and level of violent crime. We have seen that in the conventional population, there appears to be no relationship between violent or defensive beliefs described earlier and their experience with crime, as measured by their history of being arrested. While only 11 percent of the conventional sample reported having ever been arrested, a full 91 percent of the street sample reported ever being arrested. In fact, 64 of the 125 youths interviewed had spent some time incarcerated in the previous twelve months.

With the street youths interviewed for this study, we went beyond asking arrest histories and inquired into a number of actual violent behaviors. Utilizing self-reports, we tap into people's violent offending in terms of simple assaults, aggravated assaults, robberies, group conflicts, and a general violent crime measure that aggregates the previous four offenses. Respondents were asked,

> How many times in the past year did you "attack someone with weapons or a fist, or feet, so badly that they probably needed a doctor, got into a fight with someone for the hell of it; threatened or used force to get money or things from another person; got into a fight where a group of your friends was against another group?

There is much information in the interviews demonstrating that street youth are involved in a great deal of violent activity. These youths reported involvement in the past year, on average, in 6 robberies, 11.5 aggravated assaults, 42 simple assaults, and 12 group fights. The sheer volume of activity dwarfs what would be present for a general population, with street youth, on average, involved in approximately seventy-one violent incidents per youth in just the past year.

A correlational analysis of measures of violent attitudes and defensive attitudes indicates that there are significant relationships between these attitudes and several of our measures of actual violent behavior. First, we find that defensive attitudes are significantly related to participation in aggravated assaults and robberies. Second, violent attitudes are related to a higher incidence of both simple and aggravated assaults, robberies, and our measures of general violence. Thus, unlike the general population, there seems to be a consistent relationship between the approval for violence and many types of violent behavior, and there is a somewhat less generalizable relationship between defensive attitudes and violence. Thus our speculation that these street youths are more supportive of the use of violence appears to be correct, and this support for the legitimation of violence seems to be related to their violent behavior.

Conflict Scenarios

Now that we have determined that street youths appear to support and utilize violence more readily across situations than the conventional population, we move now to explore how situational context influences their decisions to move to violence. This section replicates some of the analysis reported in chapter 5 from the factorial surveys. Due to the small size of the street youth sample, the data collection was restricted to only four of the twelve scenarios, where the same four scenarios were shown to all of the respondents, choosing one scenario from each domain. The scenarios include the school yard, walking down the street, the domestic dispute, and the sporting event. In addition, a limited number of varying circumstances and intensities of conflict were presented to the respondents to enable sufficient cases in each situation for some statistical analysis. The categories for structural position were limited to lower/middle class; age was restricted to young/middle age; and intensity of the conflict was dichotomized into medium or high. Like the larger sample, each of the conditions for scenarios were randomly generated and the scenario was placed into the interview schedule. These scenarios provide us with the bases upon which to focus on the situations that engender certain styles of behavior.

Naming and Claiming

We begin by looking at what youths indicated about naming and claiming in disputes when confronted with harm doers. Recall from chapter 5 that naming is based on an assessment of how upset a person is with the potential harm doer. The street youth scored 4.8 out of 10 on the average level of upset with the potential disputant. This is somewhat lower than the 5.9 out of 10 compiled across the twelve scenarios utilized with the larger conventional sample. It also is interesting in that the level of intensity of the scenarios provided the street youths is higher. This suggests that street youths, on average, appear to be less upset than the conventional population when faced with a potential conflict. While the average level of upset is somewhat lower for street youth as a subsample of the general population, this number still indicates a moderate degree of upset and illustrates that these youths recognize that they would be in conflict with a potential harm doer in the scenario.

Like the general population, the results for the street youth indicate that the level of upset varies depending on the type of scenario. Street youths are most likely to be upset with a potential harm doer at a sporting event ($\bar{x} = 6.1$) or walking down the street ($\bar{x} = 5.4$), and least likely to be upset with the potential harm doer at a domestic dispute ($\bar{x} = 3.4$) or a school yard dispute ($\bar{x} = 4.1$). The mean levels of upset in all but the sporting event scenario were lower than those found in the general population.

Despite having lower levels of upset than their conventional counterparts, street youths were more likely to make claims against potential harm doers. A full 75 percent of the sample indicated that they would make a claim where they would ask their harm doers to stop. This number is higher than the 65 percent found in the larger conventional sample. Saying this, there is still a relationship between the level of upset and claims making. These youths were more likely to make these claims in those situations where the levels of upset were higher. For example, in the scenario with the highest average level of upset, the sporting event, 90 percent of the sample indicated that they would make a claim. For the scenario with the second highest level of upset, the street, 87 percent suggested they would make a claim. In contrast, those in conflict with potential harm doers in domestic disputes would make a claim only 49 percent of the time. The claims making at the sporting event is similar to the 87 percent of the larger sample, who also indicated that they would make a claim in this scenario. However, only 56 percent of the conventional sample suggested they would make a claim in the walking scenario. This pattern is similar for the school yard scenario, while street youths are much less likely to make a claim in domestic disputes than are their conventional counterparts.

The results of this study indicate that not only are street youths more likely to make claims, but they also are more likely to use aggression to settle these disputes. Results from the general population indicated that about 15 percent of people would use force against a potential harm doer to get them to stop. By comparison, many more street youth, about 35 percent, say they would use physical force. Again, the use of aggression would vary by the type of dispute, but street youth are more likely to say they would use physical force in situations where they are the most upset and very likely to make a claim. At the extreme, 48 percent of the street youth indicated that they would use violence against a potential harm doer in a conflict while walking on the street. This compares to the 17 percent found in the broader sample. Looking at the sport scenario, the study suggests that 40 percent of the youth would use physical force, compared to 14 percent in the conventional population. The results are higher, but not as dramatically different, at 23 percent and 31 per-

Table 7.1

Dispute Processes in High-Intensity Scenarios for Men from a General Population

Scenario	Upset Mean	Claiming (%)	Aggression (%)
School Yard	6.3	80	23
Walking	5.4	87	33
Spousal	6.5	80	56
Sporting Event	6.6	89	26

Table 7.2

Dispute Processes in High-Intensity Scenarios for Men from a Street Sample

Scenario	Upset Mean	Claiming (%)	Aggression (%)
School Yard	4.1	91	27
Walking	5.9	93	76
Spousal	4.1	90	78
Sporting Event	6.4	96	52

cent of the street respondents saying they would use physical force in the school yard and domestic conflicts, respectively, as compared to the 10 percent and 21 percent of the general population. Overall, these results present a pattern where youths may not necessarily get as upset as those in the general population, but they are more likely to make claims and more likely to move to aggression to settle their disputes.

Upset, Claiming, Aggression, and Intensity

When singling out males in the conventional sample, there is a moderate relationship between the level of upset and the intensity of the conflict (Table 7.1). This finding suggests that the naming of conflict becomes routinized so as the intensity of the conflict increases there is a tendency to view the event as potentially harmful. It appears that street youths (see Table 7.2) also routinize the naming of conflict. In all of the scenarios, the level of upset is greater in situations where the intensity of the conflict is highest. Additional analysis also indicates that street youth are more likely to be upset if the potential harm doer is a male.

Looking at claiming, however, there is little or no relationship between the intensity of the conflict and claims making. For these youths, it makes little difference if it was a high-intensity or medium-intensity situation; they were equally likely to make a claim. An exception is the domestic dispute where the level of intensity is related to claiming. Thus it appears that generally, if street youths perceive any indication of harm doing, they are likely to make a claim, although they are slightly more likely to make a claim if the potential harm is directed toward a friend rather than themselves.

The routinization of conflict is generally evident when we examine the intensity of conflict and aggression. Street youths indicate that they would be more likely to use physical force against a potential harm doer in a high-intensity situation than in a low-intensity situation. The only scenario where this pattern does not hold true is in the school yard.

The factorial survey method allows us to assess how other aspects of the situation, such as gender, social class, and age of the harm doer, may influence pathways to aggression. The results of the field study suggest that street youth, like the general population, are more likely to utilize aggression against male harm doers. The influence of structural position also varies across scenarios, as the relationship between the use of aggression varies by scenario. In the school yard and the sporting event scenario, social class makes little difference. Street youths are equally likely to aggress against lower-class and middle-class disputants. However, in the street scenario and the domestic dispute scenario, they are more likely to use aggression against lower-class harm doers. Last, the relationship between the age of the harm doer and aggression varies by scenario. Age makes little difference in the street and sporting event scenarios. In contrast, in the domestic dispute scenario, respondents indicated that they were more likely to aggress against younger harm doers, while in the school yard scenario they were more likely to utilize aggression against older disputants.

Comparing some of these results with those that we found in a larger and conventional sample from the general population, it appears that street youths would be less upset about high-intensity disputes than would be males from the general population. Yet these street kids are slightly more likely to make claims against the potential harm doers than are males in the conventional population, and much more likely to say that they would use aggression. Thus while the level of claiming is high for both samples when faced with a high-intensity situation, street youths are much more likely than males in a general population to say that they would escalate a dispute to violence.

Like the larger survey, we also asked respondents if there was anything that would stop them from using physical force if the harm doer persisted. Just as in the larger sample, there were conditions that the youths indicated they would reassess their use of violence. An example given for possible reevaluation of their aggressive decision included an apology from the harm doer, or a more reasonable offer from the harm doer. The youths indicated that they would stand by their original decisions to use violence unless peace offerings were made. Some statements from these youth for different scenarios include the following:

> No cause he wants to keep pushing me around so deserves to get a shot. Yes if people would say they are sorry (walking scenario).

> No because I'm not going to let him do that. If he politely said I'm sorry and politely asked me to leave (school scenario).

> Yes if the opposite person tried to solve it another way (domestic scenario).

> No cause he's not showing his tickct. If he shows me these seats are his I'll move. Until then get the hell out of my face (sporting event scenario).

Some respondents indicated that their aggressive response might be deterred by the potential sanctions of carrying out such an attack in a public place, particularly if they were at a large professional sporting event.

> If there was security guards around that would change it (sporting event scenario).

> There might be too many people around and I might get charged (sporting event scenario).

The respondents also were sensitive to the gender of their harm doer. These youths reported that if the scenario had substituted a female for a male harm doer, they would reevaluate their use of violence to settle the dispute.

> If she's a woman. If it was a guy he would be toast, man (school scenario).

> Yeah I don't hit women, only if she stabbed me or something I'd hit her (school scenario).

> Yes the fact she's a women I'd just restrain her (walking scenario).

Some street youth indicated that once they made a decision to use violence, nothing would make them stop. In some instances, these decisions appear to be based on the protection of females under attack from other males.

> Because I don't think that right to push a woman around. Yes if she stepped into it or if she hit me, fuck her if he kills you. That's your problem (domestic scenario).

> No classic berserk goes off when I see a guy hit a women. Its legally called temporary insanity (domestic scenario).

> No I don't think its right when a guy hits a girl (sporting event scenario).

Other street youth linked their decision to utilize violence to a need to gain retribution for the wrongs they felt had been done to them. Some examples from the survey follow:

> No cause people aren't going to push me around. It's not a crime to walk across a field in the late afternoon (school scenario).

> No cause he has no right to touch me (walking scenario).

> Buddy's touching me (walking scenario).

> No cause personally I don't like be insulted (school scenario).

> No I don't believe in being pushed around by someone. I don't like being pushed around (sporting event scenario).

> No I don't believe in being shoved around (walking scenario).

> No cause I'd be pissed off and I'd want him out of my face (sporting event scenario).

> No he started pushing me. Any natural person who gets pushed around would be pissed off especially if he wasn't doing anything (sporting event scenario).

> Because we weren't doing anything. You want to start with us, we'll start with you (walking scenario).

The common thread in these evaluations is that violence is deemed legitimate if the behavior on the part of others is identified as being inappropriate, such as showing disrespect, the violation of honor, the need to defend oneself, and other similar attributions of legitimization.

Experience with Serious Conflict

Having found considerable evidence of conflict for street youth in various domains we now would like to determine how these conflicts emerge, who is involved in these events, where they take place, and how they are resolved. The survey was structured to focus on the conflict that the respondents indicated to be the most serious.

Street youths most often identified the crime attack (33%) as the most serious type of conflict in the past year. Chapter 4 showed that this was the least prevalent form for the general population (3.6%). The extent of this problem may actually be higher, increasing to 45 percent for street youth, as they tended to indicate that their "other" conflicts also involved some sort of criminal behavior. Looking further at the most serious conflict, a significant proportion of the street sample (24%) designate a family conflict as their most serious dispute, which was the most prevalent type for a general population. Finding that there are significant family conflicts should not be a great surprise, since many street youths are drawn from homes characterized by extreme physical and emotional abuse (Baron 1997). Thus despite aggravated assaults, group fights, and robberies, a large number of these youths still view some of their family conflicts as being more serious than those they encounter on the street.

The gravity of the most serious conflict was assessed using a 1 to 7 scale, with street youth reporting an average of 4.9 across all of the conflicts. The perception of the seriousness varies across conflicts, with the crime disputes viewed as being slightly more serious than the overall average. The mean seriousness rating for the crime conflict was 5.0, while the crime threat conflict provided a 5.3 average. On the other hand, the average seriousness rating for family conflicts was somewhat lower at 4.9, while conflicts over money rated 4.2 on the seriousness scale. Overall, street youths tend to view the conflicts they are involved in as being more serious than those reported by the general population, which averaged only 3.5 out of 7.

Evidence of the seriousness of conflicts for street youth is provided by our findings that over two-thirds (68%) of conflicts progressed to violence. In comparison, recall that only 13 percent of conflicts from the larger survey escalated to violence. Supporting the idea that violence is related to seriousness, the street respondents rated those conflicts that involved violence as being more serious ($\bar{x} = 5.1$) than those that did not involve violence ($\bar{x} = 4.3$). Further, respondents were more likely to suggest that a crime had occurred if their conflict had involved violence.

The location of the dispute influences the escalation to violence. A large minority (40%) of these conflicts took place in the respondents' residence, which for these youths meant anything from their familial home, rooming house, or hotel room to an empty building taken over for squatting purposes. The remaining conflicts took place on the street, in bars, parks, malls, or other public places. Disputes that took place in the home were less likely to escalate to violence than those in public places. For example, only 61 percent of the disputes in the home progressed to violence, while over 80 percent of the conflicts that emerged on the street escalated to violence. While these numbers are much greater for our street youth sample, the tendency for disputes in public places to progress to violence is a pattern similar to that found in our conventional sample. The fact that this group spends a significant proportion of its time in public locations probably contributes to the high number of disputes in public locations.

Social Relationships

Earlier we reviewed the idea that it is important to understand the relationship and social distance between parties in crimes and disputes. Further, the role that others or "third parties" play in the resolution or escalation of the dispute must be taken into consideration. In the vast majority of the cases involving one-on-one disputes, street youth report that their combatant was well known to them (69%), or was at least an acquaintance (8%). Only 23 percent of street youth say that the person was a total stranger or someone known to them by sight only. Those youths involved in conflicts where other parties were present again for the most part knew those with whom they were in direct conflict. Only in 20 percent of the conflicts where third parties were present did the youths indicate that they did not know the other party. These numbers are more similar to those found in our conventional survey than the others we have previously examined. These results indicate that despite different structural and social locations, a great deal of conflict appears to take place among people with minimal social distance.

Yet we also discover that the nature of these disputes is different depending on the social distance of the disputants. Conflicts between strangers are more likely to involve violence than disputes that involve people who are known to one another. Over 85 percent of the conflicts involving strangers, or people the youths reported knowing only by sight, developed into violent altercations. This compares to 64 percent of those conflicts involving social relationships where the combatants were well known to each other.

The respondents indicated that for the most part their opponent had instigated the conflict (65%). Only 28 percent of street youth admitted that they were responsible for the generation of the conflict. The youths also indicated that conflicts that were started by other disputants were more likely to escalate to violence (71%) than those they themselves instigated (62%).

Most of the conflicts reported here involved others besides the two disputants. Fifty-eight percent of the respondents indicated that their conflict involved themselves, their combatant, and at least one other person. In fact, the average number of people present at these conflicts was about six. Despite the presence of others, only 7 percent say that the conflicts were instigated by third parties. However, violence is more likely when these third parties were present (73%) than when the disputants were by themselves (62%), suggesting that the pressure from others present at disputes serves to escalate conflict to violence. Bystanders also may influence the definition of the events. Findings indicate that where others were present, respondents were more likely to define the conflict as a crime. Part of this relationship may be an artifact of the violence and part from the discussion with event observers who help contextualize the activities that took place. However, third parties also can serve to reduce conflict. Reflecting the presence of others, third-party intervention is much greater in the sample of street youths than it was within the general population. In about half of the cases examined, someone intervened in the conflict. Respondents ranked those disputes where there was intervention as being more serious than those where no intervention occurred in the dispute. The most likely candidates for intervention were the police (40%) and friends (37%). This suggests that even in cases where third parties are present and available to intervene, the ultimate intervention often comes from parties not present when the conflict begins. While the police intervened in 40 percent of these conflicts, the youths themselves did not tend to reach out for their help. In only 22 percent of the cases where the police intervened did the respondents indicate that they had requested police assistance. However, it was in those conflicts ranked by the respondents to be the most serious (5.4 out of 7) that there was an intervention by police. The seriousness of the dispute was rated, on average, about one full point lower (4.5) if the police were not present.

The success of interventions in conflict is low for the street sample when considered next to the general population. Only 36 percent of the street youth felt that third-party intervention made things better. About the same number indicated that third parties made the conflict worse. Just over a quarter (28%) of the sample reported that third parties had no influence one way or another on the outcome of their conflict. Respondents noted that family members tended to be more successful in resolving disputes, while most felt that police officers made things worse. These results may reflect the seriousness of the disputes, as arrests were made by the police in 23 percent of the disputes. The prevalence of arrest increases to 58 percent of the situations when looking at situations where police become involved in the disputes. While many felt arrest made the dispute worse, it nonetheless appears to be a successful method of ending current conflicts. In 71 percent of the cases, respondents indicate that an arrest by police stopped the conflict. Yet in almost 30 percent of the cases, the conflict continued after the arrest of one of the disputants.

Perhaps reflecting the overall failure of intervention was the finding that the bulk of these youths' conflicts remained unresolved. Only 56 percent of the youths report that their most serious conflict in the past year was resolved. Further analysis conveys that 50 percent of all of the particular conflicts of street youth involve multiple incidents, demonstrating once again that there is a lack of resolution of conflicts for youth on the street. That is, half of the conflicts involved situations where adversaries had "butted heads" on more than one occasion. In fact, over one-third of these conflicts involved three or more incidents. It is clear that if the incident is not settled, it appears that it becomes likely to be drawn out over a number of occasions. The conflicts that tended to remain unresolved surrounded criminal conflicts and family disputes.

The street youth report that resolution is more likely to occur if they had instigated the conflict (66%). The likelihood of resolution drops slightly to about half of disputes resolved when other parties were viewed to have started the dispute (53%). If a dispute is ranked as being less serious, they were slightly more likely to be resolved. The presence of violence in the dispute had little effect on whether a dispute was resolved or not. Interestingly, and perhaps reflecting the ambiguous role third parties play in conflict resolution, disputes involving intervention were less likely to be resolved compared to those where there was no intervention. Thus, for street youth, intervention appears to damage the opportunity to resolve conflict.

Reflecting upon the seriousness of these disputes, the respondents indicated that in 43 percent of the cases they believed a crime had occurred. This result is more likely to be true if the dispute had taken place on the street and if police had been called in. It is also the case that youths who perceived a crime taking place in their dispute viewed the dispute as unresolved (65%), while youths who did not consider a crime involved in their dispute were more likely to report the dispute as being resolved.

Summary

This chapter has shown that street youths are heavily involved in a range of conflicts. The results comparing street youth to the conventional population have demonstrated that these youth have much more involvement in all types of conflict, particularly criminal conflicts. The majority of their conflicts escalate to violence, and their violent disputes tend to involve strangers and to emerge in public locations. The direction these conflicts take often are influenced by bystanders, and they often are repetitive and unresolved. Reflecting the seriousness of the nature of street youth conflict is the number of times police intervene. Generally we have portrayed a population that is heavily involved in repetitive violent conflict that requires the attention of the police.

This chapter has summarized how street youths, like the general public, appear to view the use of violence as being legitimate under certain conditions. However, street youths have demonstrated greater support for violence in situations where there is ambiguity toward, or disapproval of, violence from the general public. Thus street youths have appeared to condone the use of violence across a broader range of situations. This approval of violence by street youth has gone further, and it seems to be related to actual violent behaviors, ranging from robbery and group fights to aggravated assaults.

   As we have mentioned, street youths report lower levels of upset with a potential harm doer than does the general public. Like the general public, we have described how these youths' degree of naming of a dispute is linked to the intensity of the situations, but overall they remain less aroused than their conventional counterparts. However, we have found that despite lower levels of upset in a situation, street youth are more likely to make a claim and to demand an end to the offensive behavior. In fact, we have shown that any type of offensive behavior, no matter what the degree of intensity, is equally likely to meet with a claim for desistance. Street youths have reported that they are more likely to move to violence in order to satisfy their demands, although those situations with higher degrees of intensity are more likely to meet with violence. This chapter portrays a group that feels little arousal over potential harm, demands reparation, no matter how severe the harm may be, and are willing to use violence to get their way.

   It is important to note that not all disputes end in violence. These youths also have reported that apologies, offers of alternative dispute settlement, and the gender of the offender might cause them to reevaluate their use of violence. Nevertheless, these youth have said that perceptions of harm and inappropriate behavior are viewed as legitimate reasons for utilizing violence against a harm doer.

Chapter 8

Routine Conflict in Theory and Practice

Summing Up

What have we learned from our study of the social roots of violence? In the previous chapters, we have made a case for the routine nature of conflict, arguing that individuals enter into disputes with a predisposition to act in set ways. This predisposition is based on their past experience, socialization, and the cues they pick up from the situation they encounter. When in the interaction, we have argued that individuals in disputes will rely on the actions of others and will act differently depending on the domains in which the interaction occurs, but the influence of these factors, too, is routinely applied by the individuals who interact with others. The outcome of these interactions then become part of one's repertoire to guide future behavior, including the conscious choice of alternative actions in future encounters with people in similar circumstances.

We report from our study that conflict is pervasive throughout society and that there is a general tolerance for violence. This tolerance is moderated by circumstance and by the characteristics of the individuals involved in the interaction. This tolerance for violence permits the development of a set of responses that individuals use to govern their actions. We have illustrated that individuals can anticipate how they will act, including being violent, in certain conflict-based situations. The use of violence is constrained, however, by individual characteristics, the actions of others, and the suitability of violent actions in certain domains of action. For example, individuals confronted with violence in working situations are less likely to retaliate with violence than are those who face violence or criminal victimization in a public place. Part of this restraint comes from the reliance on others to intervene and part comes from the determination of likely consequences of violent actions, including, for example, the possible loss of one's job. The example illustrates that people will consider situational factors when confronted with these types of problems.

We find, as well, support for the idea that individual behavior conforms to the stages of conflict development proposed by Luckenbill and Doyle (1989). The stages of naming (or upset), claiming, and aggression demarcate steps in the escalation of conflict from the initial stages of an encounter to the engagement in violence. This escalation of conflict to violence can be stopped at different places, influenced by the extent to which individuals can resolve the conflict or use other means (such as avoidance) to escape the protagonist. The steps in the dispute process are seen as transactions between an individual and the protagonist. We illustrate, as well, that an understanding of transactions is limited without an analysis of factors that comes before the transaction, as precursors, and that follows, as aftermaths.

The precursors to the conflict include the general attitudes that individuals have about the use of violence and the definitions of the situations that allow for these types of resolution strategies. This perspective draws on the point of view that violence can be socially constructed, depending on socialization and past experience. This social construction does not deny the propensities that may come from psychological disturbance or psychopathy or other forms of emotional breakdown, but turns attention to the factors that trigger and then channel these behaviors in ways that are influenced by the social situation and the actions of others.

The aftermath of a conflict involves the deterrence and assessment of costs of the actions that took place, including evaluating the guilt or innocence of the parties involved in establishing blame for harm done. We identify, in addition, the role that coercion plays in influencing the ways in which disputes evolve. Coercive acts, we have seen, add content to the interaction through the use of threats, punishments, and physical harm. Coercive acts direct attention to the goals individuals will set when trying to get others to do things for them or to punish them for perceived transgressions. By looking at coercion, we add to the study of violence the ideas that these actions are not simply reactive, emerging in response to frustration, for example. Many acts of violence have an instrumental character by which these actions are used to obtain compliance or to punish another party. Any study of violence must attend to this instrumentalism, as it adds meaning to the ways in which many people act toward others.

The routine nature of conflict and violence can be influenced as well by the characteristics of the individuals involved. We find an important difference between the ways in which men and women react to violence and use this as a way of resolving their conflicts. Men are more likely to express the view that violence is a reasonable option for them, especially when confronted with an aggressive person. Women, who are as likely to be involved in a conflict as men, are less likely to choose violent responses as a means of dealing with disputes with other individuals. This pattern holds true even when others are violent to them in the first place. Women suggest that while they are likely to be upset, violence is not often an option for them. These results are consistent with what we witness in everyday life, with men more likely to be involved in violent acts. Aggression is considered a real option in the male world—there is legitimacy and support for this action among peers. Even so, the use of violence by males is situational, as we have seen with the major differences in the ways in which males (including our sample of street youth) are likely to deal with other males versus women in aggressive situations. It is not gender alone, however, that determines violent outcomes. Again, the context, including the apparent costs of acting in violent ways, becomes an important part of the ways in which individuals manage their interactions.

The drama of everyday life then is a complex array of cultural meanings, structural influences, and coercive actions all set in time and space. To understand violence, it is not enough to look at individual actors or single events. We have shown that people in the general population can construct specific responses to questions that ask about violence, and that they can attach conditions under which they themselves would use this behavior. While this in itself is not that surprising, it contradicts much of the way in which criminology has viewed violence, particularly in its almost exclusive focus on the aggressive personality of offenders. This research underlines the importance of understanding more about how the complexity of social interaction can contribute to violence. We need to examine the totality of meaning that emerges from interaction that directs individuals to act in a certain way.

Elements of Routine Conflict Theory

In this book, we have addressed a number of theoretical views that focus on the social roots of violence. Our study has operationalized a wide range of factors that contribute to an integrated view of the social roots of violence. We target micro-level behavior in contrast to the approaches that have utilized integrated perspectives to look at the more macro influences on interpersonal violence (see, for example, Miethe and Meier 1994). We also look at both a general population sample and a sample of street kids and find common elements in our research relating to routine expectations about violence and the domain specific factors that restrict or promote this violence.

We have suggested that the aggression theories that have promoted the view that violence derives from frustration or from a need to directly retaliate for an attack unrealistically focus too much attention on the offender and not enough on the situation. Further, we argued that while self-control theories allow us to add information about opportunity for violence into the equation, knowing that someone has low self-control does not tell us enough about the ways in which individuals make their choices about how to deal with conflict under the circumstances they confront in daily living.

We prefer to look at the situationally defined interactions where meaning is created through the active participation of all parties. This approach draws from the observations of Goffman (1974) and Luckenbill (1977) about the ways in which interactions become more than simply actions of one party or the other in isolation. Rather, interactions take on additional meaning as a result of the ways in which individuals react to others and to the situation. We draw as well on the literature that talks about codified or routine approaches to conflict, whereby individuals manage the complexity of the world through a set of specific expectations or repertoires of behavior that they use to guide them through daily living (Barley 1986). This approach attends to the concerns about how people come together in social interactions that are dynamic, influenced by the situational factors that appear in the location in which they take place. These interactions may evolve into conflicts and disputes that pass through a series of prescribed steps: precursors, transactions, and aftermaths (Sacco and Kennedy 1996; Miethe and Meier 1994).

Within the transaction itself, the escalation to violence evolves from naming to claiming to aggression (Luckenbill and Doyle 1989). These processes provide a way of looking at the active rather than passive states of individuals' involvement in violent behavior, as characterized by routine activities theory.

How do we summarize the elements of routine conflict theory? We propose a series of interrelated processes that comprise the theoretical foundations of this perspective. "Routines" that define the ways in which individuals approach conflict are based on people's values founded in their assessments of the acceptability of violence in different situations. The legitimation of violence clearly varies by individual and by group. However, we have established that violence is not a rarely valued outcome. Instead, we have demonstrated that violence is legitimated throughout society in a wide variety of situations and circumstances. These routines that define how to manage conflict and violent responses are not static, however, but are influenced by a number of other factors. These include structural elements, past experience, context, the role of third parties, and the content of the interaction, particularly whether or not the actions contained in the interaction are coercive. We can summarize the ways in which these elements of routine conflict are likely to be formed and to influence interaction.

Socialization provides individuals in society with a prescribed set of actions that they use to guide their behavior in conflict situations. We have referred to these as "routine conflicts." People develop these routines over time through interaction with others and through a learning process that creates in individuals expectations about what actions will occur in certain situations. This repertoire is not fixed, however, as we can see in the alternatives within the scenarios that we offered to our respondents. What is important, though, is the observation that there is a fairly consistent response across individuals concerning how they process choices and respond to the increased intensity of conflict through stronger reactions.

One choice that people can make in reacting to others' behavior is to use violence. Violence can be the routine of choice for individuals who are limited in their repertoires or who face violence in daily living, as illustrated in our street sample. However, exercising these violent routines, even for those who are in confrontational situations on a regular basis, is dependent on how the interaction evolves and on the actions of others in the situation. In other words, the violence is not inevitable or predetermined, but its manifestation is made more likely as individuals run out of choices of ways of dealing with conflict in nonviolent ways.

Structural factors that affect routines include the characteristics of the respondents, most particularly gender. Males are more likely to use violent repertoires and are most likely to use them against other males. We have seen that the repertoires that individuals develop in dealing with others can be heavily influenced by their judgments of who the other person in the interaction is and what they do to provoke a response in the individual. Routine conflict choices among males compared to females are more likely to include aggressive responses, helping us explain why males are more likely to be involved in criminal violence.

Past experience will influence the ways in which individuals adjust their expectations about violent interaction. While self-control can obviously be important in influencing the ways in which individuals learn from their experiences, it is not obvious from this research that it will preclude any further learning after routine conflict approaches are learned in early life. We have taken a strong position on the importance of individuals developing routines, based on what they have experienced in the past. This perspective is consistent with the observations made about the cycle of violence, where people learn to be violent by watching others who are violent, particularly in family situations. We extend this observation about cycles of violence to the general population, who also have violent repertoires, not necessarily learned from direct experience. These repertoires are developed through exposure to media or to stories told by others who have experienced these violent situations. While not likely to be invoked among individuals who experience only low-intensity conflicts on a daily basis, these repertoires are considered part of one's choices when dealing with daily life. In more highly confrontational situations, these violent repertoires are more likely to be invoked.

Third parties are important for defining what an acceptable routine conflict approach in interaction is. Third parties also can play a role in influencing the outcome of the conflict, including escalating the problem to a higher level of intensity. They provide feedback to others about how their behavior with the protagonist is viewed, and they can be important in influencing the choices that are made. Third parties, such as the police, also can be used to preclude the use of a violent repertoire, as individuals who see great risk in being aggressive use formal agents as a way of dealing with highly confrontational situations. For individuals who see that the police is not an option for them to turn to, the violent repertoire is more likely to be invoked.

We cannot consider routine conflict without the all-important influence of context. The distinctions in the use of repertoires across domains illustrate that individuals learn not only how to act when confronted by certain violent acts but that this is tempered by the situation in which this act takes place. While we have chosen to look at four different domains—work, street, leisure, and the home—it is obvious that finer distinctions can be made to illustrate the important effects that context can have on conflict behavior. It is also evident that certain contexts are predefined as being more likely to enhance conflict and to require a violent response. We see this in the research that has been conducted on bar behavior. But the less obvious examples of highly violent encounters include some family and work situations. By examining how routine conflicts develop in these contexts and by increasing our understanding of how individuals exercise the choice of repertoires that they use in handling others, we can gain greater insight into family or workplace violence.

That there are consistent steps individuals go through in defining the situation supports the view that individuals are continuously sorting through cues in interaction to guide their choices. But this processing of cues does not imply that individuals always begin from scratch in their social behavior. The cues attach to repertoires. They trigger set responses. Through the naming, claiming, and aggression process, we can see this as a narrowing of choices as the intensity of conflict increases.

Prescriptions for Restricting Violent Routines

These elements of routine conflict theory make it clear that the motiveless violence that was described in chapter 1 is not likely to occur very often.

While violence can be random, it is more likely that it emerges as a consequence of daily routines that script the actions and responses of individuals involved in these behaviors. Understanding how these routines are developed suggests ways in which we can act to curtail violent acts. Even stranger violence is unlikely to occur out of a particular context, where routines are clearly identified and context plays an important part in influencing outcomes.

The propositions laid out earlier are not offered in a predictive form, although we suggest that the ways in which these actions combine in daily transactions routinize ways of acting. It is clear that the dynamics of these interactions make it hard for us to "predict" the outcomes of interaction that will be violent. As our research shows, there are an infinite number of situations and a wide array of responses depending on characteristics of interactants and contexts. But this is not to say that this approach cannot offer clear prescriptions for curtailing violence. These prescriptions can be presented in a summary form as follows:

1. We need to spend more effort discussing the deleterious effects of violence in society and reduce this as an option for people in dealing with others. In other words, efforts made to delegitimize violence can provide an important basis for changing society's orientation that allows violence as an option in certain situations. Our research supports the views of advocates of media reform that direct attention to reducing the amount and character of violence on television and in movies. These media depictions of violence promote a set of routines that becomes a part of the ways in which people see themselves dealing with others—ways that may lead to greater levels of violence and greater harm.

2. It is important, in this context, that we direct attention to the ways in which individuals manage conflict in family situations and use violence as a way of attaining certain outcomes from others in these situations. The strong efforts to change people's views of the harmfulness of family violence support attempts to remove violence as an alternative in dealing with family members.

3. What about violence as self-defense? Many of the scenarios support the view that people will reluctantly respond to violence in kind but not in situations where there are clear alternatives offered through access to supervisors, security, or police. While it seems naïve to suggest that people not respond to threatening offenders as a way of protecting themselves, there is some question about the suitability of self-defense that encourages individuals to take the law into their own hands, through self-arming, for instance. The response to violence through violence encourages a legitimation of aggressive repertoires. There is enough evidence to show that this has the effect of raising the intensity of violence in society. We need to

pay greater attention to this issue in an effort to understand how self-help provides a means by which individuals protect themselves and their property.

4. We need to promote greater efforts to control the ways in which individuals use their temper to get others to act in particular ways. This directs attention at efforts to remove coercion from interaction, including domestic relations where coercion becomes an important part of the abuse cycle. The particular targets for these programs are violent offenders who are encouraged to seek alternatives to using their anger to control or hurt other people. These programs also have proven useful in dealing with young people who need to learn about alternatives to aggression in trying to attain their goals. Our approach broadens the view of anger management as a way of dealing with frustration to one that looks at encouraging individuals to assess how they are likely to deal with different situations and respond in nonviolent or nonangry ways.

5. Greater efforts must be made to show people in communities that they have options available to them to resolve minor disputes that have the potential to become more serious. The increased attention by police and other agencies to integrate mediation programs into a crime control strategy acknowledges the intense level of conflict and potential harm that can emerge from unresolved minor conflicts.

In our sample of street kids, we see the increase in violence that accompanies oppositional environments. Increasing people's choices may involve reducing some of the factors that limit their opportunities. As William Julius Wilson has recently pointed out, a major solution to deal with the problems of disadvantaged youth is to provide them with jobs. This solution not only directs attention to the need to provide these people with greater wealth, but it also involves providing people with more skills to see alternatives and increase problem solving. This can only have a positive effect on the ways in which they make choices, including the choice to be nonviolent, in their daily interaction.

Future Research

Future research on the elements of routine conflict needs to examine the ways in which we can include aspects of this in our examination of victim surveys and in the elements of smaller scale ethnographic studies that look at violent behavior in some detail. Victim surveys provide a great deal of information about crime out of the context in which this crime takes place. We need to place more emphasis on the dynamics of the whole situation in these studies, rather than using them as simple counts of the extent of harm done to certain groups in society. We have seen some efforts to improve victim surveys along these lines. For example, there have been changes in the National Crime Victimization Survey in the ways in which it documents the factors that surround sexual assault. A contextualization of crime types will improve our ability to understand how these behaviors develop and what can be done to prevent them.

It is important to consider our research as well in the context of victimization research that has looked at the experiences of victims of violence. Ellingworth, Farrell, and Pease (1995) suggest that victims of violence may be chronically revictimized. How does victimization influence individuals' responses to routine conflict? We believe that answers may be found in further studies of victimology that examine the emotional, behavioral, and social costs of victimization. Often, victims suffer long-term effects of their injuries, including difficulties sleeping and problems with social interaction, indicating that the social factors that promote violence in the first instance do not disappear after the first instance. These repetitions of victimization are not clearly understood, although they appear to reside in the trauma that comes from victimization leading to stress disorders where victims come to believe that they are losing control over their lives, making it difficult to escape their persecutors or the situations that enhance violence (Friedman and Tucker 1997). How do repertoires influence not only how individuals become violent but the long-term consequence of these violent repertoires on those who become victims? The effects of victimization and multiple victimization on routine conflict processes need to be assessed.

We also would encourage more studies along the lines of the work reported by Stephen Baron in chapter 7. Future studies should examine the direct effect of individual choices on violent outcomes in the context of how others in the interaction behave. Detailed work can be done in looking at bars, workplaces, and family situations that helps define how routine conflict emerges and that helps define the behavioral outcomes in these situations. In these studies, all actors (not just offenders) should be studied. Ethnographies have the advantage of providing through observation and testimony of actors direct links between expectations and actual behavior, links that are sometimes difficult to make when using survey data.

Last, it is important that we pay attention to the social structural factors that may work to increase the conditions under which these types of violent acts occur. The study of macrosociological forces, such as unemployment and poverty, needs to be added to the analysis of the ways in which individuals form routine conflict responses to situations that they find threatening, or where they use violence to control others in the face of inadequate resources that make nonviolent choices less attractive. In this context, the work of

Miethe and Meier (1994) is informative in providing clues about the ways in which we can develop a micro/macro analysis that attends to conditions that encourage violence. John Hagan and his associates (see, for example, Hagan, MacMillan, and Wheaton 1996) explore the importance of social capital for enhancing individual resources and for allowing individuals' greater choice in managing their environment. The idea that social capital can expand or restrict individuals' choices conforms nicely to the idea that violence emerges out of routines that influence the formation of choices to engage or to not engage in violence.

The contribution of this book, we believe, is its emphasis on looking for the roots of violence in everyday life and suggesting that we all (to a greater or lesser degree) see aggression, where push comes to shove, is a choice that we can make in resolving conflict. This routine conflict can be understood as the exercise of choice, dependent on circumstance. The focus on choice and the emphasis on context offer an alternative to theories that look only at offenders or concentrate on extreme violence. The challenge in the future is to more fully document how routine conflict strategies that are violent can be substituted by nonviolent options, reducing harm and improving social relations. We hope that this work provides a first step in addressing these concerns and serves as a basis for future thinking about violence as a socially imbedded phenomenon.

Appendix A
Social Conflict Project:
Sampling Report for Alberta

Introduction

The Conflict Project survey data collection in Alberta was conducted by the Population Research Laboratory (PRL). This report describes the sampling design, data collection method, and weighting technique used with the data set.

Sampling Design

1. *Main Features of Design*:

A. Province of Alberta delineated into three areas for telephone interviewing.
   1. City of Edmonton
   2. City of Calgary
   3. Remainder of the Province (Other Alberta)

B. Two-stage selection process.
   1. Selection of households
   2. Selection of respondent within each household

To permit the analysis of each area as a separate entity, a minimum sample size of 400 or more for each area of the province was deemed necessary.

The population universe designated for telephone interviewing was all persons eighteen years of age or older who, at the time of the survey, were living in a dwelling unit in Alberta that could be contacted by direct dialing. From this population, three samples were drawn to cover the province: the City of Edmonton, the City of Calgary, and the remainder of the region.

The samples were drawn from updated computer files of five-digit telephone banks covering all of Alberta. From these files a simple random sample of banks with replacement was drawn for each area, appending a random number between 00 and 99 to each number selected. All duplicate numbers were discarded.[1]

Nursing homes and temporary residences were deleted from the sample. Within the household, one eligible person was selected as the respondent for the interview.

A respondent was selected within each household on the basis of gender, using the following selection guidelines to ensure an equal selection of male and female participants:[2]

1. The dwelling unit must be the person's usual place of residence and he or she must be eighteen years of age or older.
2. If an adult male answers the phone and is willing to be interviewed, he is the respondent.
3. If an adult female answers the phone and there is an adult male present who is willing to be interviewed, interview the male. If the male is not willing to be interviewed, and the female is willing, interview the female.
4. If an adult female answers the phone and there is no adult male present, choose her as the respondent.

Table A.1 shows the final breakdown of the telephone samples by the gender of the respondent.

Table A.1
Unweighted Sample Sizes in Alberta by Area and Gender

Gender	Edmonton		Calgary		Other Alberta		Total	
	N	*(%)*	*N*	*(%)*	*N*	*(%)*	*N*	*(%)*
Male	202	49.8	212	50.4	203	49.4	617	49.8
Female	204	50.2	209	49.6	208	50.6	621	50.2
Total	406	100.0	421	100.0	411	100.0	1238	100.0

The Questionnaire

The questionnaire contained a wide variety of questions pertaining to the study's objectives and was pretested by professional interviewers in both Edmonton and Winnipeg. From the findings of the pretest, modifications were made to the questionnaire before the main interviewing began. All questions were submitted to a University of Alberta research ethics committee to ensure suitability for administration to the general public.

Data Collection

The interviewing began on February 6 and was completed by the middle of March. Ninety-seven percent of the telephoning was completed from a supervised location at the University of Alberta. Interviewing was conducted every day of the week throughout the data collection period. A total of thirty-three trained interviewers completed the interviewing.

If the interviewers were unsuccessful in establishing contact on their first call, they were to make at least ten callback attempts before declaring a telephone number "no contact." Upon making contact, the interviewer identified herself or himself,[3] verified the telephone number, and then asked the screening questions for selecting the respondent. Before administering the questionnaire, the interviewer advised the respondents that their participation was voluntary, that their responses would be kept completely confidential, and that they could stop the interview at any time.[4] Twenty-nine percent of the respondents were recontacted by the supervisors for interviewing validation. No significant discrepancies or irregularities were found.

Refusal call sheets were scrutinized by the supervisors to ascertain whether a second call should be made. Details of the refusal outlining the exact words used by the householder were recorded by the interviewers. In the majority of cases, the refusal was not definite and final. Only the most experienced interviewers made callbacks to request an interview again and to explain further the purpose of the survey. Forty-two percent of householders who were called back agreed to do an interview.[5] Because of the high number of householders who agreed to an interview after a subsequent call, this recontacting procedure is a very worthwhile endeavour. The response rate for the whole sample was 74.7%.

Table A.2 shows the breakdown of the initial sample selections.

Calculation of Weights

The final sample obtained for each area is not proportional to the Alberta population it represents. For instance, Edmonton is oversampled. Edmonton makes up only 25 percent of the Alberta population but has 33 per-

Table A.2
Breakdown Dispositions of Original Samples, Alberta 1994

	Other				Other			
	EDM N	CAL N	AB N	Total N	EDM (%)	CAL (%)	AB (%)	Total (%)
Samples as Drawn	1,200	1,125	1,117	3,234	100.0	100.0	100.0	100.0
Deduct:								
Nonresidential or Ineligible	−273	−282	−223	−778	25.2	26.9	20.3	24.1
Not in Service	−264	−182	−347	−793	24.4	17.3	31.5	24.5
Second Residence	−1	−1	−4	−6	00.1	00.1	00.4	00.2
Eligible Sheets	546	585	526	1657	50.4	55.7	47.8	51.2
Corrected Sample Breakdown								
Completed Interviews	406	421	411	1,238	74.4	72.0	78.1	74.7
Incomplete Interviews	10	5	5	20	01.8	00.9	01.0	01.2
Refusals	89	120	69	278	16.3	20.5	13.1	16.8
Language Problems	20	12	3	35	0.37	02.1	00.6	02.1
Other	0	0	0	0	00.0	00.0	00.0	00.0
No Contacts	21	27	38	86	03.8	04.6	07.2	05.2
Total	546	585	526	1,657	100.0	100.0	100.0	100.0

Table A.3
Calculation of Weights for Alberta

Sample Area	1991 Population 20+ Years	Percentage[1] of Population	Sample Size	Percentage of Sample	Weight Factor	Weighted Sample
Edmonton	447,120	25.31	406	32.79	0.771787	313
Calgary	511,660	28.96	421	34.01	0.851724	359
Other Alberta	807,750	45.73	411	33.20	1.37732	566
Total	1,766,530	100.00	1,238	100.00		1,238

Note: [1]Statistics Canada, "Census of Canada, 1991, Profile of Census Divisions and Subdivisions in Alberta—Part A." Catalogue 95–372, Ottawa.

cent of the interviews. Therefore, in order to combine the samples for a provincial sample, weighting is necessary.[6] Table A.3 contains the information used to calculate the weights.

The Data

The raw data file exists as an eighty column/record rectangular data set. The data was tabulated and cleaned using the OSIRIS and SPSSx statistical packages, and special programs developed by the PRL. The data cleaning process included wildcode, discrepant value, and consistency checks. The resultant data set contains 224 (plus three created variables—PINEORES, PINEOSPO, and WT) variables for each case. There is a total of 1,238 cases with seven records per case. A SPSSx system file with labels has been created to analyze the data.

Telephone Introduction Sheet 1994

1. Hello, I'm calling (long distance) on behalf of the Population Research Lab at the University of Alberta. My name is _____ (full name or Mrs. XXXXX)

2. I have dialed XXX–XXXX. Is this correct?

3. Your telephone number was selected at random by computer.

4. Just a moment of your time to explain why I'm calling.

5. The lab at the university is currently conducting an important study on conflict situations with other people in everyday life.

6. To ensure that we have a 50–50 split of men and women in the study, please tell me how many men and women age eighteen or over live at this number.

   NUMBER OF MEN _____   NUMBER OF WOMEN _____

7. Does this total include yourself as a member of this household over the age of eighteen?

8. We don't always interview the person who answers the phone. For this interview I need to speak to one of the adult male members of the household. May I speak to (the male member/a male member who is available)?

   REQUESTING AN INTERVIEW WITH THE
   PERSON WHO ANSWERS THE PHONE

9. I would like to interview you. I'm hoping that now is a good time for you. Your opinions are very important for the research that is being done at the University of Alberta.

10. Before we start, I'd like to assure you that your participation is voluntary and that any information you provide will be kept confidential and anonymous. If there are any questions that you do not wish to answer, please feel free to point these out to me and we'll go on to the next question. You of course have the right to terminate the interview at any time.

(OPTIONAL READ)

We do not need your name, so no one will know your answers to these questions. If you have any questions about the survey, you can call the Study Supervisor (in Edmonton) at 492–2505 for further information.

Appendix B
Social Conflict Project:
Sampling Report for Manitoba

Introduction

The Conflict Project survey data collection in Manitoba was conducted by the Winnipeg Area Study (WAS). This report describes the sampling design, data collection method, and weighting technique used with the data set.

Sampling Design

1. *Main Features of Design*:

A. Province of Manitoba delineated into two areas for telephone interviewing.
    1. City of Winnipeg
    2. Remainder of the Province (Other Manitoba)

B. Two-stage selection process.
    1. Selection of households
    2. Selection of respondent within each household

To permit the analysis of each area as a separate entity, a minimum sample size of 250 or more for each area of the province was deemed necessary.

The population universe designated for telephone interviewing was all persons eighteen years of age or older who, at the time of the survey, were living in a dwelling unit in Manitoba that could be contacted by direct dialing. From this population, two samples were drawn to cover the province: the City of Winnipeg and the remainder of the province.

The samples were drawn from updated computer files of five-digit telephone banks covering all of Manitoba. From these files a simple random sample of banks with replacement was drawn for each area, appending a random number between 00 and 99 to each number selected. All duplicate numbers were discarded.

Nursing homes and temporary residences were deleted from the sample. Within the household, one eligible person was selected as the respondent for the interview.

A random predesignation of each household as either male or female was recorded on the front of the interview.[1]

Interviewers were instructed as follows:

1. If the person answering the phone is the gender specified for that phone number, only that person can be interviewed.
2. If the person answering the phone is not of the gender specified for that phone number, ask the person to choose for you an individual of the appropriate gender in the household. No guidelines are to be given for this selection. No substitutions are permitted if the selected person refuses. If the person is not at home, or for some reason is not available at that time, every effort must be made to set up an interview appointment.
3. If a person of the gender specified for that phone number does not live there, the respondent must be the person who answers the phone.

An eligible respondent also was someone eighteen years of age or older, and who resided at that address.

Table B.1 shows the final breakdown of the telephone samples by the gender of the respondent.

Table B.1
Unweighted Sample Sizes in Manitoba, by Area and Gender

Gender	Winnipeg		Other Manitoba		Total	
	N	(%)	N	(%)	N	(%)
Male	255	45.2	134	53.6	389	47.8
Female	309	54.8	116	46.4	425	52.2
Total	564	100.0	250	100.0	814	100.0

The Questionnaire

The questionnaire contained a wide variety of questions pertaining to the study's objectives and was pretested by professional interviewers in both Edmonton and Winnipeg. From the findings of the pretest, modifications were made to the questionnaire before the main interviewing began. All questions were submitted to a University of Manitoba research ethics committee to ensure suitability for administration to the general public.

Data Collection

The interviewing began on February 2 and was completed by the end of March. Interviewing was conducted every day of the week throughout the data collection period. A total of twenty-two trained interviewers completed the interviewing.

If the interviewers were unsuccessful in establishing contact on their first call, they were to make at least ten callback attempts before declaring a telephone number "no contact." Upon making contact, the interviewer identified herself or himself, verified the telephone number, and then asked the screening questions for selecting the respondent. Before administering the questionnaire, the interviewer advised the respondents that their participation was voluntary, that their responses would be kept completely confidential, and that they could stop the interview at any time.[2] Twenty-nine percent of the respondents were recontacted by the supervisors for interviewing validation. No significant discrepancies or irregularities were found.

The response rate for the Manitoba sample was 76.6%, based on completed interviews divided by eligible interviews (completed plus refused). The completion rate in Winnipeg was 74.2% versus 82.5% elsewhere in Manitoba. Table B.2 shows the breakdown of the refusals and replacements to the Manitoba sample.

Calculation of Weights

The final sample obtained for each area is not proportional to the Manitoba population it represents. For instance, Winnipeg is oversampled. Winnipeg makes up only 62 percent of the Manitoba population but has 69 percent of the interviews. Therefore, in order to combine the samples for a provincial sample, weighting is necessary.[3] Table B.3 contains the information used to calculate the weights.

The Data

The data file exists as an SPSS Portable data set. The data was tabulated and cleaned using the SPSS/PC Data Entry II statistical package. The data

Table B.2
Refusals and Replacements to the Manitoba Sample by Area

	Winnipeg N	Other Manitoba N	Total N	Winnipeg (%)	Other Manitoba (%)	Total (%)
Completed Interviews	564	250	814	65.0	72.9	67.2
Refusals	196	053	249	22.6	15.5	20.6
Language Problems	039	008	047	04.5	02.3	03.9
Health, Age	065	026	091	07.5	07.6	07.5
Other	004	006	010	00.5	01.7	00.8
Total	868	343	1,211	100.0	100.0	100.0

Table B.3
Calculation of Weights for Manitoba

Sample Area	1991 Population 20+ Years	Percentage[1] of Population	Sample Size	Percentage of Sample	Weight Factor	Weighted Sample
Winnipeg	476,045	61.66	564	69.29	0.889883	502
Other Manitoba	295,960	38.34	250	30.71	1.248453	312
Total	772,005	100.00	814	100.00		814

Note: [1]Statistics Canada, "Census of Canada, 1991, Profile of Census Divisions and Subdivisions in Manitoba—Part A." Catalogue 95–358, Ottawa.

cleaning process included wildcode, discrepant value, and consistency checks. There is a total of 814 cases. An SPSS Portable file with labels has been created to analyze the data.

Telephone Introduction Sheet 1994

1. Hello, I'm calling (long distance) on behalf of the Winnipeg Area Study at the University of Manitoba. My name is _____ (full name or Mrs. XXXXX)

2. I have dialled XXX–XXXX. Is this correct?

3. Your telephone number was selected at random by computer.

4. Just a moment of your time to explain why I'm calling.

5. The university is currently conducting an important study on conflict situations with other people in everyday life.

6. To ensure that we have a 50–50 split of men and women in the study, please tell me how many men and women age eighteen or over live at this number.

    NUMBER OF MEN _____   NUMBER OF WOMEN _____

7. Does this total include yourself as a member of this household over the age of eighteen?

8. We don't always interview the person who answers the phone. For this interview I need to speak to one of the adult male members of the household. May I speak to (the male member/a male member who is available)?

REQUESTING AN INTERVIEW WITH THE
PERSON WHO ANSWERS THE PHONE

9. I would like to interview you. I'm hoping that now is a good time for you. Your opinions are very important for the research that is being done at the University of Manitoba.

10. Before we start, I'd like to assure you that your participation is voluntary and that any information you provide will be kept confidential and anonymous. If there are any questions that you do not wish to answer, please feel free to point these out to me and we'll go on to the next question. You of course have the right to terminate the interview at any time.

(OPTIONAL READ)

We do not need your name, so no one will know your answers to these questions. If you have any questions about the survey, you can call the Study Supervisor (in Winnipeg) at 474–9198 for further information.

Appendix C
Combining the Alberta and Manitoba Samples

The final sample obtained for each province is not proportional to the population it represents.[1,2] For instance, Manitoba is oversampled. Manitoba makes up only 30 percent of the combined Alberta and Manitoba population but has 39 percent of the interviews. Therefore, in order to combine the samples for an interprovincial sample, weighting is necessary.[3] Table C.1 contains the information used to calculate the weights. The interprovincial weighting variable is stored in the data file as WT2.

Table C.1
Weighting of Combined Sample

Sample Area	1991 Population 20+ Years	Percentage[1] of Population	Sample Size	Percentage of Sample	Weight Factor	Weighted Sample
Alberta	1,766,530	69.59	1,238	60.33	1.153489	1,428
Manitoba	772,005	30.41	814	39.67	0.766574	624
Total	2,538,535	100.00	2,052	100.00		2,052

Appendix D
Interview Instrument

ALBERTA/MANITOBA CONFLICT PROJECT SURVEY, 1994

INTERVIEWER NAME _____

START TIME (24 hr.clock) ____|____|____|____

FIRST OF ALL, COULD YOU GIVE ME SOME INFORMATION ABOUT THIS HOUSEHOLD?

1. How long have you lived in this residence?

   ___ ___ years or ___ ___ months

2. Including yourself, how many persons altogether live here, related to you or related to you or not?

   Adults _____ (18+)
   Children _____ (Under 18)
   TOTAL _____

3. Now a list of the members of this household. To make it easier, I'm going to ask for the first name of each member. (START WITH RESPONDENT ON LINE 1)

RELATIONSHIP TO RESPONDENT	01	RSPDNT	02	SPOUSE/COMPANION
	03	SON	04	DAUGHTER
	05	MOTHER	06	FATHER
	07	SIBLING	08	RELATIVE
	09	FRIEND	10	OTHER
			99	NA
			00	NR

FIRST NAME	SEX 1 MALE 2 FEMALE	AGE	RELATIONSHIP TO
(1)_____	|_____|_____		RESPONDENT 01
(2)_____	|_____|_____	|_____	
(3)_____	|_____|_____	|_____	
(4)_____	|_____|_____	|_____	
(5)_____	|_____|_____	|_____	
(6)_____	|_____|_____	|_____	
(7)_____	|_____|_____	|_____	
(8)_____	|_____|_____	|_____	
(9)_____	|_____|_____	|_____	
(10)_____	|_____|_____	|_____	

4. In what type of building do you live (e.g., house, apartment, townhouse)?

Single house (incl. basement suite)..................1
Duplex—side by side 2
Duplex—one above the other..........................3
Row/town house 4
Apartment less than 5 stories (incl. 4 plex)......5
Apartment with 5 or more stories.....................6
House attached to a nonresidential structure....7
Mobile home..8

5. What is your current living arrangement? (READ RESPONSES, CODE LOWEST NUMBER)

Now married and living with spouse 1
Common-law relationship or live-in partner....2
Single—never married 3
Divorced...4
Separated 5
Widowed..6

NOW SOME QUESTIONS ABOUT CRIME
AND THE CRIMINAL JUSTICE SYSTEM.

6. Compared to TWO years ago, would you say that crime in your NEIGH-BORHOOD has:

Increased 3
Remained the same, or 2
Decreased...1
    DK...8

7. How safe do you feel or *would* you feel walking alone in your neighborhood after dark? Would you feel:

Very safe 1
Reasonably safe 2
Somewhat unsafe, or 3
Very unsafe 4
    DK...8

8. In general, would you say that the sentences handed down by the Canadian criminal courts are:

Too severe...3
About right, or 2
Not severe enough 1
    DK...8

9. Alberta (Manitoba) has several programs where crime victims may meet with the person who committed the crime, in the presence of a trained mediator, to let this person know how the crime affected him or her and to work out a plan for repayment of losses.

A. Suppose you were the victim of a nonviolent property crime committed by a young adult (18 to 26). How likely would you be to participate in a program like this? Would you say:

Very likely.......................................4
Likely 3
Unlikely, or 2
Very unlikely...................................1
    DK..8

B. Now suppose you were the victim of a nonviolent property crime committed by a juvenile (17 years or less). How likely would you be to participate in a mediation program? Would you say:

Very likely..4
Likely...3
Unlikely, or...2
Very unlikely..1
　　DK...8

10. Next, suppose that you are away, your home is burglarized, and $1,100 worth of property is stolen. The burglar has one previous conviction for a similar offense. In addition to a sentence of three years on probation, which would you prefer:

Repayment of $1,100 to *you*, or..............1
4 months in jail for the burglar...............2
Both (volunteered and insistent).............3
　　DK..8

11. For the greatest impact on reducing crime, should additional money be spent on:

More prisons or...1
Education, job training,
and community programs...........................2
　　Both (volunteered and insistent).....3
　　DK...8

12. For the next questions, please answer *yes* or *no*.

Suppose you are a witness to an incident where one man punches an adult male stranger. Would you approve if the adult stranger

A. was in a protest march showing opposition to the other man's views?

Yes..1
No...2
　　DK..8

B. was drunk and bumped into the man and his wife on the street?

Yes..1
No...2
　　DK..8

C. had hit the man's child after the child accidentally damaged the stranger's car?

Yes..1

No...2

DK...8

D. was beating up a woman *and* the man saw it?

Yes...1

No...2

DK...8

E. had broken into the man's house?

Yes...1

No...2

DK...8

Next, would you approve of a police officer striking an adult male citizen

F. if the male citizen had said vulgar and obscene things to the police officer?

Yes...1

No...2

DK...8

G. if the male citizen was being questioned as a suspect in a murder case?

Yes...1

No...2

DK...8

H. if the male citizen was attempting to escape from custody?

Yes...1

No...2

DK...8

I. if the male citizen was attacking the police officer with his fists?

Yes...1

No...2

DK...8

13. For the next questions, please answer *strongly agree, somewhat agree, somewhat disagree,* or *strongly disagree.*

A. I often act on impulse (spur of the moment) without stopping to think. (Optional read)

Strongly agree...................................1
Somewhat agree.............................2
Somewhat disagree, or....................3
Strongly disagree 4
    DK.....................................8

B. I often devote much thought and effort to preparing for the future. (Optional read)

STRONGLY AGREE			STRONGLY DISAGREE	DK
1	2	3	4	8

C. I often do whatever brings me pleasure here and now, even at the cost of some distant goal. (Optional read)

STRONGLY AGREE			STRONGLY DISAGREE	DK
1	2	3	4	8

D. I'm more concerned with what happens to me in the short run than in the long run. (Optional read)

STRONGLY AGREE			STRONGLY DISAGREE	DK
1	2	3	4	8

E. I frequently try to avoid projects that I know will be difficult. (Optional read)

STRONGLY AGREE			STRONGLY DISAGREE	DK
1	2	3	4	8

F. When things get complicated, I tend to quit or withdraw. (Optional read)

STRONGLY AGREE			STRONGLY DISAGREE	DK
1	2	3	4	8

G. The things in life that are easiest to do bring me the most pleasure. (Optional read)

STRONGLY AGREE			STRONGLY DISAGREE	DK
1	2	3	4	8

H. I dislike really hard tasks that stretch my abilities to the limit. (Optional read)

STRONGLY AGREE			STRONGLY DISAGREE	DK
1	2	3	4	8

I. I almost always feel better when I am on the move than when I am sitting and thinking. (Optional read)

STRONGLY AGREE			STRONGLY DISAGREE	DK
1	2	3	4	8

J. I would rather go out and do things than sit at home and read. (Optional read)

STRONGLY AGREE			STRONGLY DISAGREE	DK
1	2	3	4	8

K. I seem to have more energy and a greater need for physical activities than most people my age. (Optional read)

STRONGLY AGREE			STRONGLY DISAGREE	DK
1	2	3	4	8

L. I try to look out for myself first (even if it means making things difficult for other people). (Optional read)

STRONGLY AGREE			STRONGLY DISAGREE	DK
1	2	3	4	8

NEXT, A FEW QUESTIONS ABOUT THE POLICE.

14. During the past twelve months, did you come into contact with the police

	Yes	No
A. for a public information session such as Neighborhood Watch?	1	2
B. for a traffic violation?	1	2
C. as a victim of a crime?	1	2

D. as a witness to a crime?	1	22
E. for committing a crime?	1	2 2
(specify crime below)		

15. Have you *ever* been arrested?

Yes..1
No..2 (GO TO QUESTION 16)
What was the reason?
(specify; last time if more than once)

_____

_____

16. In the past *two years*, have you done any of the following things to protect *yourself* or *your property* from crime? Have you

	Yes	No
A. changed your routine, activities,or avoided certain places?	1	2
B. installed new locks?	1	2
C. installed burglar alarms?	1	2
D. taken a self-defense course?	1	2
E. changed your phone number?	1	2
F. obtained a dog?	1	2
G. obtained a gun?	1	2

NEXT, SOME QUESTIONS ABOUT SOCIAL CONFLICTS.

Everyone gets into conflicts with other people once in a while. Some disputes are very serious and some are not. I am going to ask you about some conflicts that you may have had with other adults (over eighteen) in the *last twelve months*.

17. First, (in the last *twelve months*) were you involved in a crime attack? (actual robbery, or assault)?

Yes..1
No..2 (GO TO QUESTION 18)
A. Who was involved?

_____

_____

18. . . . (in the last *12 months*) were you involved in a situation where a crime attack (robbery, assault) was threatened but not carried out?

    Yes..1
    No...2 (GO TO QUESTION 19)
    A. Who was involved?

    _____

    _____

19. . . . (in the last *12 months*) were you involved in an argument over money?

    Yes..1
    No...2 (GO TO QUESTION 20)
    A. Who was involved?

    _____

    _____

20. . . . (in the last *12 months*) were you involved in an argument with a landlord?

    Yes..1
    No...2 (GO TO QUESTION 21)
    A. Who was involved?

    _____

    _____

21. . . . (in the last *12 months*) were you involved in an argument with a neighbor?

    Yes..1
    No...2 (GO TO QUESTION 22)
    A. Who was involved?

    _____

    _____

22. . . . (in the last *12 months*) were you involved in a conflict in the family?

    Yes..1
    No...2 (GO TO QUESTION 23)
    A. What was this person's relationship to you?

    _____

    _____

23. . . . (in the last *12 months*) were you involved in any other conflict?

    Yes 1
    No .... 2 (GO TO QUESTION 24)
    A. Who was involved?

    _____
    _____

Now, a quick review of the conflicts. You've indicated you were involved in (name the types of conflict) in the past year.

24. (Interviewer: Check if yes)

	Yes	
a crime attack	___	
a crime threat	___	
an argument over money	___	
an argument with a landlord	___	(IF R ANSWERED **ONE** TYPE, GO TO QUESTION 27)
an argument with a neighbor	___	
a conflict in the family	___	
another conflict	___	
No conflicts (none of the above)	___	(IF NONE, GO TO QUESTION 47, PAGE XXX)

25. Which *one* of these (Question 24) was the most serious conflict?

    crime attack 1
    crime threat 2
    argument over money 3
    argument with landlord 4
    argument with neighbor......................... 5
    conflict in the family 6
    other conflict 7 7
        DK 8

26. Briefly, would you describe what happened and why it was the most serious conflict?

    _____
    _____
    _____

27. I would like to ask you a few questions about the _____:
    (name most serious type of conflict).

    Where did this incident take place? (check all that apply)

    A. at home   ____
    B. at work   ____
    C. at school   ____
    D. on sidewalk/street/highway   ____
    E. in a restaurant or bar   ____
    F. in a park or recreation area ____
    G. elsewhere   ____

              (specify) _____

28. Thinking back to the circumstances of the dispute, who started the conflict?

    you (self)..1
    the other person, or................................2
    a third party (someone else)...................3

29. How many people were involved, not including yourself?

    ___ ___ (Number) (If more than one person, go to Question 32)

        DK 98

30. How well did you know this person? Would you say:

    Well known...1
    Casual acquaintance ....2 (GO TO QUESTION 34)
    Known by sight only, or ....3 (GO TO QUESTION 34)
    You did not know him/her......................4 (GO TO QUESTION 34)

31. What was the person's relationship to you?

    Spouse...1 (GO TO QUESTION 34)
    Ex-spouse..2 (GO TO QUESTION 34)
    Other relative ....3 (GO TO QUESTION 34)
    Friend..4 (GO TO QUESTION 34)
    Neighbor ....5 (GO TO QUESTION 34)
    Other ....6 (GO TO QUESTION 34)

              (specify) _____

32. Did you know any of these people?

    Yes 1
    No ....2 (GO TO QUESTION 34)
        DK...8 (GO TO QUESTION 34)

33. What was their relationship to you? (check all that apply)

    Spouse ....____
    Ex-spouse ....____
    Other relative(s) ....____
    Friend(s) ....____
    Neighbor(s) ....____
    Other . . . .____

        (specify) _____

34. Was this the first and only time this incident happened, or did it happen
    more often?

    only time...................................1
    two times 2
    three or more times.....................3
        DK 8

35. Was there any violence in the dispute?

    Yes 1
    No ....2 (GO TO QUESTION 37)

36. Would you briefly describe what violence happened?

    _____
    _____
    _____
    _____

37. Was the dispute resolved (ended)?

    Yes 1
    No ....2 (GO TO QUESTION 39)

38. Briefly, what helped to resolve the conflict?

    _____
    _____
    _____
    _____ (GO TO QUESTION 40)

39. Has this dispute escalated (gotten worse) over time?

    No ....2 (GO TO QUESTION 40)
    Yes 1

    If yes, in what ways has the dispute escalated?

    _____

    _____

40. Sometimes other parties intervene in conflicts, for example, friends, neighbors, police, lawyers, or others.

    A. Did anyone else intervene in your conflict?

    Yes ....
    No ....2 (GO TO QUESTION 41)

    B. Who was principally involved in intervening in your conflict? (circle one)

friend	01
neighbor	02
stranger	03
police	04
lawyer	05
social worker	06
insurance company	07
family member	08
other	09

    (specify) _____

    C. Did they (person in B) make things *better*, *worse*, or did things stay the *same*?

    Better..1
    Worse, or..2
    Same 3
    DK...8

41. Did you call the police?

    Yes 1
    No 2

42. Did the police come?

    Yes 1
    No 2

43. Do you think a crime occurred?

    Yes 1
    No 2

44. Did the police make an arrest?

    Yes 1
    No ....2 GO TO QUESTION 46)

45. Do you think the arrest stopped the conflict from continuing?

    Yes 1
    No 2

46. Overall, on a 7–point scale from 1 = *not at all serious* to 7 = *extremely serious*, how serious would you say this conflict was/is?

Not at all serious					Extremely Serious		DK
1	2	3	4	5	6	7	8

47. What is the most serious thing that has ever happened to you that could be considered a crime?

    (Interviewer: *one* response only. Do not read.)

		Your approximate age when this happened?
Sexual assault (rape, attempted rape, molesting, attempted molesting)	01	__ __
Robbery / Attempt (face-to-face threat or assault with a weapon and theft of property. If there was no weapon, no attack or any threat of attack classify elsewhere.)	02	__ __
Assault (face-to-face threat or assault with a weapon but no theft of property or attempt)	03	__ __

    Break and Enter / Attempt
    (illegal entry or attempt

into your residence or any other
building on your property).........................04   __ __

Motor vehicle theft / attempt
(theft or attempted theft of
motor vehicle or part) 05   __ __

Theft of personal property / attempt
(money or other personal property
was taken or attempted to be taken)..........06   __ __

Theft of household property / attempt.......07   __ __

Vandalism (something was damaged) 08   __ __

Other 87   __ __

    (Specify)

_____

_____

Not applicable/never a victim of crime 99

NEXT I AM GOING TO ASK YOU SOME QUESTIONS ABOUT SOME TYPES OF CONFLICTS. I WILL DESCRIBE A BRIEF SCE- NARIO AND THEN I WILL ASK YOU TO CONSIDER WHAT YOU WOULD DO IN THE SITUATION.

(INSERT QUESTIONS FROM FOUR VIGNETTES)
See Appendix E

NOW WE WOULD LIKE TO ASK YOU A FEW QUESTIONS ABOUT YOUR LIFESTYLE.

48. People participate in a variety of evening activities outside of their home. On average, how many times *a month* do you go out during the *evening* to do the following activities?

	No. of times per month
A. Work nights, attend night classes, go to meetings, or do volunteer work	__ __
B. Go to restaurants, movies, or the theater	__ __

C. Go to bars or pubs   ___ ___

D. Go out for sports, exercise, or recreational activities   ___ ___

E. Shop in the evening   ___ ___

F. Go to bingo   ___ ___

G. Go to a casino or to play VLTs (Video Lottery Terminals)   ___ ___

H. Visit relatives or friends in their own homes   ___ ___

I. Other evening activities not already mentioned   ___ ___

THE NEXT QUESTIONS ARE ABOUT SMOKING.

49. At the present time, do you smoke cigarettes *daily*, *occasionally*, or *not at all*?

Daily 1
Occasionally 2
Not at all ....3 (GO TO QUESTION 51)

50. About how many cigarettes do you smoke each day? ___ ___ ___

51. Do you smoke pipes, cigars, or cigarillos *daily*, *occasionally*, or *not at all*?

Daily 1
Occasionally 2
Not at all 3

NOW A QUESTION ABOUT DRINKING.

52. In the past twelve months, how often, on average, did you drink any alcoholic beverages such as beer, wine, or liquor? (use list to probe if necessary)

Never...00
Every day 01

6 days a week 02
5–6 days a week 03
5 days a week 04
4–5 days a week 05
4 days a week 06
3–4 days a week 07
3 days a week 08
2–3 days a week 09
2 days a week 10
1–2 days a week 11
1 day a week (4 days/month) 12
3–4 days a month....................................13
3 days a month...14
2–3 days a month....................................15
2 days a month...16
1–2 days a month....................................17
once a month 18 18
less than once a month 19
   DK...98

THE NEXT QUESTIONS ARE ABOUT TRAVELLING IN A CAR, TRUCK, OR OTHER MOTOR VEHICLE.

53. At the present time, do you wear a seat belt during *every trip, occasionally*, or *not at all*?

Every trip...1
Occasionally 2
Not at all 3

54. In the last twelve months have you driven a car, truck, or other motor vehicle?

Yes. 1
No . . . . 2 (GO TO QUESTION 56)

55. How often would you say that you would exceed the speed limit by 20km/hr whenever you could get away with it? Would you say:
Always...1
Occasionally, or 2
Never..3
DK..8

THE NEXT QUESTIONS ARE ABOUT RISK TAKING.

56. For these questions, please answer *strongly agree, somewhat agree, somewhat disagree,* or *strongly disagree.*

  A. I like to test myself every now and then by doing something a little risky. (Optional read)

     Strongly agree...................................1
     Somewhat agree..............................2
     Somewhat disagree, or.....................3
     Strongly disagree............................4
        DK...8

  B. Sometimes I will take a risk just for the fun of it. (Optional read)

STRONGLY AGREE			STRONGLY DISAGREE	DK
1	2	3	4	8

  C. Excitement and adventure are more important to me than security. (Optional read)

STRONGLY AGREE			STRONGLY DISAGREE	DK
1	2	3	4	8

  D. If I had a choice, I would always do something physical rather than something mental. (Optional read)

STRONGLY AGREE			STRONGLY DISAGREE	DK
1	2	3	4	8

  E. I'm not very sympathetic to other people, even when they are having problems. (Optional read)

STRONGLY AGREE			STRONGLY DISAGREE	DK
1	2	3	4	8

  F. If things I do upset people, it's their problem not mine. (Optional read)

STRONGLY AGREE			STRONGLY DISAGREE	DK
1	2	3	4	8

G. I will try to get the things I want, even when I know it's causing problems for other people. (Optional read)

STRONGLY AGREE			STRONGLY DISAGREE	DK
1	2	3	4	8

H. I lose my temper pretty easily. (Optional read)

STRONGLY AGREE			STRONGLY DISAGREE	DK
1	2	3	4	8

I. Often, when I'm angry at people, I feel more like hurting them than talking to them about why I am angry. (Optional read)

STRONGLY AGREE			STRONGLY DISAGREE	DK
1	2	3	4	8

J. When I'm really angry, other people better stay away from me. (Optional read)

STRONGLY AGREE			STRONGLY DISAGREE	DK
1	2	3	4	8

K. When I have a serious disagreement with someone, it's usually hard for me to talk calmly about it without getting upset. (Optional read)

STRONGLY AGREE			STRONGLY DISAGREE	DK
1	2	3	4	8

NOW SOME QUESTIONS ABOUT SOCIAL CONTACTS.

57. Of your relatives, excluding those who live in your household, how many do you see at least once a month?

___ ___ ___

DK.....................998

58. Of your friends, excluding any who may live in your household, how many do you see at least once a month?

___ ___ ___

DK....................998

59. Who would you turn to first (not including your spouse or children at home) if:

A. you needed help for work in your home or garden?

Father 1
Mother...2
Friend..3
Neighbor 4
Other 5
    (specify) _____
       DK......................................8

B. you had to borrow a large sum ($500) of money?

Father 1
Mother...2
Friend..3
Neighbor 4
Bank..5
Other 6
    (specify) _____
       DK......................................8

C. you were depressed?

Father 1
Mother...2
Friend..3
Neighbor 4
Physician...5
Other 6
    (specify) _____
       DK......................................8

D. you had to make an important personal decision and needed advice?

Father 1
Mother...2
Friend..3
Neighbor 4
Bank..5
Other 6
    (specify) _____
       DK......................................8

THESE FINAL QUESTIONS WILL GIVE US A BETTER PICTURE OF THE PEOPLE WHO TOOK PART IN THE STUDY.

60. In 1993, how many months were you employed full time? Part time?

    A. Months FULL TIME   ___ ___
    B. Months PART TIME   ___ ___

61. What is your current employment or work situation? For each of the following, please tell me if it applies to you.
    (Have respondent answer each question.)

	YES	NO	NA
A. Employed full time	1	2	
B. Employed part time	1	2	

    (ASK c if R is AGE 45+ and *not* employed full time)

C. Retired (no job at all)	1	2	9

    (If respondent answers yes to any of the above, go to question 62; otherwise, continue.)

D. Unemployed (out of work and looking for work)	1	2	9
E. Never in the labor force	1	2	9

62. People also do a variety of other types of work, even though it may not involve a paid job. For each of the following, please tell me if it applies to you.

    (Record "shared," only if volunteered.)

	YES	NO	SHARED
A. Mainly responsible for housework	1	2	3
B. Mainly responsible for raising a child or children	1	2	3
C. Taking care of some other dependent person (elder, disabled, grandchild)	1	2	3
D. Currently going to school or studying in some program	1	2	
E. Doing some volunteer work	1	2	

(If never in the labor force, go to question 66.)

63. What kind of work do/did you normally do? That is, what is/was your job title?

_____

64. What does/did that job involve? (describe)

_____

_____

65. What kind of business or organization (do/did) you work for? What (does/did) your employer do or make?

    INDUSTRY _____

(*Note:* **Ask in question 66 if R is married/common law; all others to to question 71.**)

66. Please tell me which of the following work situations apply to your spouse/partner at the present time. Is he/she:

    (Have respondent answer each question.)

	YES	NO	NA
A. Employed full time	1	2	
B. Employed part time	1	2	

    (**ASK in C if spouse/partner is age 45+ and *not* employed full time.**)

    | C. Retired (no job at all) | 1 | 2 | 9 |

    (**If respondent answers yes to any of the previous questions, go to question 67; otherwise, continue.**)

    | D. Unemployed (out of work and looking for work) | 1 | 2 | 9 |
    | E. Never in the labor force | 1 | 2 | 9 |

67. People also do a variety of other types of work, even though it may not involve a paid job. For each of the following, please tell me if it applies to your spouse/partner.

    (Record **"shared"** only if volunteered.)

	YES	NO	SHARED
A. Mainly responsible for housework	1	2	3
B. Mainly responsible for raising a child or children	1	2	3
C. Taking care of some other dependent person (elder, disabled, grandchild)	1	2	3
D. Currently going to school or studying in some program	1	2	
E. Doing some volunteer work	1	2	

(*Note:* **If spouse/partner was never in the labor force, go to question 71.**)

68. What kind of work does/did your spouse/partner normally do? That is, what is/was his/her job title?

_____

69. What does/did that job involve? (describe)

_____

_____

70. What kind of place (does/did) he/she work for?

Industry _____

NEXT, CONSIDERING EDUCATION . . .

71. What is your highest level of education (includes complete and incomplete)? (Circle category below.)

72. What is your spouse's/partner's highest level of education (includes complete and incomplete)? (Circle category below.)

	Respdt	Spouse/Partner
No Schooling	01	01
Elementary School		
Incomplete	02	02
Complete	03	03
Junior High School		
Incomplete	04	04
Complete	05	05
High School		
Incomplete	06	06
Complete (GED)	07	07
Non-University (Voc/Tech, Nursing Schools)		
Incomplete	08	08
Complete	09	09
University		
Incomplete	10	10
Diploma/Certificate (e.g., hygienists)	11	11
Bachelor's Degree	12	12
Professional Degree	13	13
(vets, physicians, dentists, lawyers)		

Master's Degree 14	14
Doctorate 15	15
NO SPOUSE ....—	99
DK ....—	98

73. Where were your parents born? Were they: (read responses)

    Both born outside of Canada? 1
    One born in Canada? 2
    Both born in Canada? 3
    DK...8

74. How would you describe your ethnic identity? (Examples of ethnic or cultural groups include: Ukrainian, German, Japanese, etc.)

    _____

75. To what ethnic group(s) did your father's side of the family belong?

    _____

    DK...98

76. To what ethnic group(s) did your mother's side of the family belong?

    _____

    DK...98

77. Would you say you (and your family) are *better off* or *worse off* or just the *same* financially than you were a year ago?

    Better off..1
    Worse off 3
    Same 2
       DK...8

78. Now, looking ahead—do you think that a *year from now* you (and your family) will be *better off* or *worse off* or just about the *same* financially than you are now?

    Better off..1
    Worse off 3
    Same 2
       DK...8

79. What is the total income of *all members of this household* for this past year *before* taxes and deductions? (Circle the corresponding category number.)

No income	00	36,000–37,999	17
Under $ 6,000	01	38,000–39,999	18
6,000– 7,999	02	40,000–44,999	19
8,000– 9,999	03	45,000–49,999	20
10,000–11,999	04	50,000–54,999	21
12,000–13,999	05	55,000–59,999	22
14,000–15,999	06	60,000–64,999	23
16,000–17,999	07	65,000–69,999	24
18,000–19,999	08	70,000–74,999	25
20,000–21,999	09	75,000–79,999	26
22,000–23,999	10	80,000–84,999	27
24,000–25,999	11	85,000–89,999	28
26,000–27,999	12	90,000–94,999	29
28,000–29,999	13	95,000–99,999	30
30,000–31,999	14	100,000+	31
32,000–33,999	15	DK	98
34,000–35,999	16	NR	99

80. What is your own total *individual* income for this past year *before* taxes and deductions? (Circle the corresponding category number.)

No income	00	36,000–37,999	17
Under $ 6,000	01	38,000–39,999	18
6,000– 7,999	02	40,000–44,999	19
8,000– 9,999	03	45,000–49,999	20
10,000–11,999	04	50,000–54,999	21
12,000–13,999	05	55,000–59,999	22
14,000–15,999	06	60,000 64,999	23
16,000–17,999	07	65,000–69,999	24
18,000–19,999	08	70,000–74,999	25
20,000–21,999	09	75,000–79,999	26
22,000–23,999	10	80,000–84,999	27
24,000–25,999	11	85,000–89,999	28
26,000–27,999	12	90,000–94,999	29
28,000–29,999	13	95,000–99,999	30
30,000–31,999	14	100,000+	31
32,000–33,999	15	DK	98
34,000–35,999	16	NR	99

81. Do you (or your spouse) presently own or rent your residence?

own 1
rent 2

82. A. If an election were held today, how would you vote *federally*?

   Liberal 1
   New Democratic Party 2
   Progressive Conservative 3
   Reform Party 4
   Wouldn't vote 5
   Not eligible.......................................6
   Other
   　　(Specify) _____ 7
   　　DK...8

   B. If an election were held today, how would you vote *provincially*?

   Liberal..1
   New Democrats 2
   Progressive Conservative 3
   Wouldn't vote 4
   Not eligible.......................................5
   Other
   　　(Specify) _____ 6
   　　DK...7

83. We'd like to know whether we reach people from all areas in Alberta/Manitoba. Can you please tell me your postal code?

   __ __ __ / __ __ __

   NR 000 000
   DK 888 888

84. Finally, if we want to talk to you (or a member of your family) again with some follow-up questions, may we call you?

   Yes 1
   No 2

85. In the spring we mail out a summary report of the study findings. Would you like a copy of the report? If so, may I have your complete name and mailing address?

   _____
   _____
   _____

Thank you for taking the time to do this interview.

86. Finish time (24-hour clock) ____|____|____|____

THIS PAGE IS TO BE COMPLETED BY THE INTERVIEWER.

87. Quality of interview:

High quality 1
Adequate 2
Questionable 3

88. Respondent's cooperation:

Cooperative..1
Indifferent 2
Uncooperative..3

89. Did you ask spouse/partner or others for privacy?

Yes ....1 (Continue)
No ....2 (GO TO 90)
NA...9 (GO TO 90)

If yes, did the person(s) comply?

Yes 1
No 2

90. Sources of interview interference, if any? (Complete for all categories.)

	Yes	No
Alcohol	1	2
Language	1	2
Age	1	2
Illness	1	2
Noise	1	2
Presence of spouse	1	2
Presence of children	1	2
Presence of others	1	2
Phone calls (call waiting)	1	2
Other	1	2

(specify) _____

| THUMBNAIL SKETCH |

91. Anything about the respondent or the interview situation that seems important?

_____

_____

_____

_____

I declare that this interview was conducted in accordance with the interviewing and sampling instructions given by the Population Research Laboratory, Alberta/Winnipeg Area Study, Winnipeg. I agree that the content of all of the respondent's responses will be kept confidential.

_____

(Interviewer's signature)

Appendix E
Scenarios

Each respondent received one scenario from each domain: work, street, family, and leisure. Conditions were varied across respondents providing differences by structural position, object of attack, intensity, and presence of others. Respondents were asked standard questions on each vignette concerning the level of upset, nature of claim, and the use of force in response to the approach by the other.

1. Suppose (you/you and a friend) are walking across a field at a public school in late afternoon. The school yard is (practically empty/very crowded). A (male/female)(lower class/middle class/wealthy) looking (youth/35-year-old/elderly person) (tells [you/your friend] /yells insulting comments at [you/your friend]/ pushes at [you/your friend]) to get you off of the field.

2. Next, let's say (you were working alone/you were at work with several coworkers). A stranger comes into the office to register a complaint. The stranger is a (lower class/middle class/wealthy) looking (18-year-old/35-year-old/elderly) (male/female). (He/she) walks in and (loudly tells/yells insulting comments at/pushes) (you/your coworker) saying the product is defective.

3. Next, suppose (you/you and a friend) are waiting at a counter for a clerk to help you with a purchase and the store is (practically empty/very crowded). A (lower class/middle class/wealthy) looking (18-year-old/35-

year-old/elderly) (man/woman) (cuts in/yells at [you/your friend] to cut in/pushes[you/your friend] to cut in) front saying (he/she) is late for an appointment.

4. Next, suppose (you/you and a friend) are passing by a local convenience store on an afternoon walk. The street is (practically empty/very crowded). Suddenly, a person (yells out loudly/yells out insulting comments/steps out and pushes) at (you/your friend). This person is a (lower class/middle class/wealthy) looking (18-year-old/35-year-old/elderly) (man/woman).

5. Now, suppose (you/you and a friend) are on your way home from a restaurant. You are walking and the street is (practically empty/very crowded). Suddenly, a (lower class/middle class/wealthy) looking (18-year-old/35-year-old/elderly)(man/woman) steps in front of (you/your friend). (He/she) (tells [you/your friend]/yells insulting comments and tells [you/your friend]/pushes and tells [you/your friend]) to hand over your money.

6. Next, suppose (you/you and a friend) are out for a drive in a car and the street is (practically empty/very crowded). Suddenly, while stopped for a light, the car behind you fails to stop and strikes your car, giving you a jolt. The other driver is a (lower class/middle class/wealthy) looking (18-year-old/35-year-old/elderly)(man/woman). After looking at the damage, the other driver (calls [you/your friend]/yells insulting comments saying [you are/your friend is]/pushes and calls [you are/your friend is]) a menace to traffic for stopping abruptly.

7. Now, let's say you've gone (alone/with your spouse or a friend) out to dinner at a friend's home. They are having a (small/very large) dinner party. One couple, whom you've never met before, is having a fight. A (lower class/middle class/wealthy) looking (18-year-old/35-year-old/elderly) (man/woman) is (yelling at/yelling at and insulting/pushing) (his/her) spouse or partner.

8. Now, suppose you've gone (alone/with friends) to a school play. It is a (small/very large) affair. As the play is about to start, a child has become separated from his/her guardian and the child accidentally bumps into (you/your friend). The child's supervisor at the play is a (lower class/middle class/wealthy) looking (18-year-old/35-year-old/elderly) (man/woman). This person comes over and (yells at/yells insulting comments at/hits) the child.

9. Now, let's say you're (alone/with friends) at home and your neighbor is having a (small/very large) party. Suppose your neighbor is a (lower class/middle class/wealthy) looking (18-year-old/35-year-old/elderly) (man/woman). If it was late evening and the noise from the party was (loud/getting worse/getting worse inside and outside their home).

10. Next, suppose you are (alone/with friends) at a sporting event and you are sitting in seats that a stranger comes up to and claims, without showing a ticket. The seats around you are (practically empty/very crowded). The stranger (tells/yells insulting names/pushes)(you/your friend) to leave. The other person is a (lower class/middle class/wealthy) looking (18-year-old/35-year-old/elderly)(man/woman).

11. Next, let's say you have gone out (alone/with friends) to a neighborhood pub or bar and you are using a Video Lottery Terminal. The bar is (practically empty/very crowded). A stranger comes over and wants to use the machine. Without waiting (his/her) turn they (tell/yell insulting names/yell insulting names and pushes)(you/your friend) to leave. The stranger is a (lower class/middle class/wealthy) looking (18-year-old/35-year-old/elderly)(man/woman).

12. Finally, suppose (you/you and a friend) are on vacation out of town taking a late-night walk. The street is (practically empty/very crowded). Suddenly, a person steps in front of you bumping into (you/your friend). This person is a (lower class/middle class/wealthy) looking (18-year-old/35-year-old/elderly)(man/woman). After looking at (you/your friend), (he/she) (calls [you/your friend]/yells insulting names at [you/your friend] and calls [you/your friend]/pushes and calls [you/your friend]) a lousy tourist and says to get off the street and go back to your hotel.

Notes

Chapter 1

1. While this may be true in Canada, police response in the United States will be less certain, given legal ambiguities across jurisdictions and because of organizational fragmentation.

Chapter 2

1. Part of this discussion is drawn from Forde and Kennedy (1997) "Risky Lifestyles, Routine Activities, and the General Theory of Crime." *Justice Quarterly* 14: 265–94. Reprinted with permission.

2. See, for example, articles included in a reader edited by Gottfredson and Hirschi (1994) that look at family, accidents, drugs, and alcohol; and Keane, Maxim, and Teevan (1993) for a test of behavioral aspects of self-control.

Chapter 3

1. In a more recent development, however, a civil trial brought against Goetz by a survivor of his shooting resulted in a $43 million settlement for pain and suffering brought about by the debilitation that came from the bullet wound (Nossiter 1996). While the criminal jury felt that the circumstances of the case warranted the use of violence, the civil jury clearly did not. In these considerations, it is not obvious that these decisions are made on a global basis. As the Goetz case illustrates, judgments about the event can evolve as more information becomes available, or as different perspectives of the event are considered.

Chapter 4

1. Note that in chapter 7 we will provide results from a study of street youth, which was designed supplementary to this research.

2. Lavrakas (1993) discusses how telephone surveys, through an understanding of social factors related to answering the telephone, may achieve results with quality that is as high as in-person interviews.

3. The details on the sample sizes and weighting are included as technical Appendices A and B.

4. Note that the University of Manitoba Ethics Committee on research involving human subjects asked what we would do if we encountered "potential or actual child abuse." If we did, we would have been obligated by law to call the police to inform them about the details of the interview and the potential of child abuse. To maintain a promise that all responses to questions would be treated as confidential, and to satisfy the concern of the University Ethics Committee, we restricted questions to conflicts that involved only adults by specifically asking about conflict with another adult age eighteen or over.

5. We expect that there will be some telescoping of responses, as in victimization surveys, where respondents may report on events outside of the desired one-year time frame. This is most likely to occur in reports of serious violent crimes that may have occurred at an earlier point in time. Similarly, there will be some error in the classification of events as crimes, since respondents will provide their own interpretation of events rather than a legal definition of events.

6. We are not able to assess the degree of the severity of violence, nor whether hospitalization was involved, because of space limitations in the questionnaire.

Chapter 5

1. Theories of dispute processes also may include an additional step in the sequence of disputes: naming, blaming, and claiming (see Felstiner et al. 1980–1981). The distinction between naming and blaming was developed in organizational psychology where it may be difficult to identify the potential harm doer. Luckenbill and Doyle (1989) indicate that it is not necessary to distinguish between naming and blaming when the focus is on interpersonal transactions where the harm doer is present (p. 423).

2. We wish to thank David Luckenbill for his suggestions on scenarios to study conflict. This section is based on Kennedy and Forde (1996) "Pathways to Aggression: A Factorial Survey of 'Routine Conflict.'" *Journal of Quantitative Criminology* 12(4): 417–38. Reprinted with permission.

3. For example, intensity may increase as talked to, yelled at, and pushed.

4. Note that the N from each of the scenarios is unequal, due to nonresponse from some households, ranging from 658 to 713. Since scenarios were randomly assigned, this is not expected to bias the results of the factorial survey. Nonresponse on items in each scenario also was less than 1 percent for all of the scenarios.

5. The category is coded 1 if it is yes, with all others coded 0, except the vacation scenario, which is coded −1.

Chapter 6

1. When the expected number of persons in a cross tabulation drops below ten, we suppress analysis of that cell as unreliable and report the results as "too few cases to estimate."

Chapter 7

1. This chapter was written specifically for this book by Stephen Baron. Funding for this research came in part from the University of Windsor Research Board and the Social Sciences and Humanities Research Council of Canada. Thanks to Leslie Kennedy, David Forde, and Darrell Langevin and the Boyle Street Co-op for their assistance.

2. Both the researchers and their university's ethics committee concluded that it was improper for a male researcher to ask female respondents questions of this nature. Methodologically, the nature of the data collection (relatively short, "one shot" interviews in a semipublic place) may have affected the validity and reliability of responses from female respondents to these questions. One potential solution was to eliminate these questions. However, past research suggested that these types of variables were particularly important in explaining the backgrounds and behaviors of both male and female street youth. Since the lack of financial support precluded hiring a female interviewer, and these questions could not be eliminated, the decision was made to restrict the sample to male street youth. Due to concerns raised in the ethics review about the sensitive nature of some of the questions bearing on physical and sexual victimization, as well as other issues raised in the interviews, including substance abuse, a referral list of relevant social service agencies was a constant companion of the researcher. Despite the sensitivity of a number of the questions, the interviews proceeded without issue, and the respondents seemed at ease in responding to the interview questions.

3. Upon assent, they were supplied with informed consent forms outlining study goals and apprising them of their rights within the interview situation. Subjects were notified that they were not obliged to respond to any of the questions, and they were provided with the option to withdraw from the interview at any time. None of the youth exercised this power.

Appendix A

1. Fifty percent of the numbers selected represented valid residential households.

2. Past surveys have indicated that 60 percent of the time the first household contact is female. The selection process works best when calls are made in the evening and on weekends.

3. Six of the thirty-three interviewers were male.

4. See end of Appendix A for the telephone introduction used.

5. Overall, 478 householders were classified as initially refusing. Two hundred completed an interview after subsequent calls.

6. If the samples are analyzed individually, then no weighting is necessary, for example, if the researcher is only interested in the Edmonton responses. In the SPSSx system file the weight variable is WT. By default, the weighting is on and is turned off with the procedure command, WEIGHT OFF. To turn weighting back on insert, WEIGHT BY WT.

Appendix B

1. Past surveys have indicated that the selection process works best when calls are made in the evening and on weekends.

2. See Appendix for the telephone introduction used.

3. If the samples are analyzed individually, then no weighting is necessary, for example, if the researcher is only interested in the Winnipeg responses. In the SPSSx system file the weight variable is WT. By default, the weighting is on and is turned off with the procedure command, WEIGHT OFF. To turn weighting back on, insert WEIGHT BY WT.

Appendix C

1. Statistics Canada, "Census of Canada, 1991, Profile of Census Divisions and Subdivisions in Alberta—Part A." Catalogue 95–372, Ottawa.

2. Statistics Canada, "Census of Canada, 1991 Profile of Census Divisions and Subdivisions in Manitoba—Part A." Catalogue 95–358, Ottawa.

3. If the provincial samples are analyzed individually, then weighting by WT is sufficient, for example, if the researcher is only interested in the Manitoba responses. If the data are to be examined as a combined sample, WEIGHT BY WT2.

References

Adler, F., G. O. W. Mueller, and W. S. Laufer. 1994. *Criminology*, Second Edition. New York: McGraw-Hill.

Agnew, R. S. 1992. "Foundation for a General Strain Theory of Crime and Delinquency." *Criminology* 30(1): 47–87.

Agnew, R. S., and D. M. Petersen. 1989. "Leisure and Delinquency." *Social Problems* 36(4): 332–50.

Akers, R. L. 1991. "Self-control as a General Theory of Crime." *Journal of Quantitative Criminology* 7: 201–11.

Anderson, E. 1994. "The Code of the Streets." *Atlantic Monthly* (May): 81–94.

Arneklev, B. J., et al. 1993. "Low Self-Control and Imprudent Behavior." *Journal of Quantitative Criminology* 9: 225–47.

Babbie, E. 1989. *The Practice of Social Research* (5th ed.). Belmont, Calif.: Wadsworth.

Ball–Rokeach, S. 1973. "Values and Violence: A Test of the Subculture of Violence Thesis." *American Sociological Review* 38: 736–49.

Bandura, A. 1973. *Aggression: A Social Learning Analysis.* Englewood Cliffs: Prentice Hall.

———. 1986. *Social Foundations of Thought and Action: A Social Cognitive Theory.* Englewood Cliffs: Prentice Hall.

Barley, S. R. 1986. "Technology as an Occasion for Structuring: Evidence from Observations of CT Scanners and the Social Order of Radiology Departments." *Administrative Science Quarterly* 31(1): 78–108.

Barlow, H. D. 1991. "Explaining Crime and Analogous Acts, or the Unrestrained Will Grab at Pleasure Whenever They Can." *Journal of Criminal Law and Criminology* 82: 229–42.

Baron, R. A., and D. R. Richardson. 1994. *Human Aggression (2d edition)*. New York: Plenum.

Baron, S. W. 1997. "Canadian Male Street Skinheads: Street Gang or Sreet Terrorists?" *Canadian Review of Sociology and Anthropology* 34(1): 125–154.

———. 1997. "Risky Lifestyles and the Link Between Offending and Victimization." *Studies on Crime and Crime Prevention* 6: 53–72.

———. 1995. "Serious Offenders." In J. H. Creechan, and R.A. Silverman, eds., *Canadian Delinquency*. Toronto: Prentice Hall.

Berkowitz, L. 1993. *Aggression: Its Causes, Consequences, and Control*. New York: McGraw-Hill.

———. 1989. "Frustration–Aggression Hypothesis: Examination and Reformulation." *Psychological Bulletin* 106: 59–73.

———. 1988. "Frustrations, Appraisals, and Aversively Stimulated Aggression." *Aggressive Behavior* 14(1): 3–11.

Bernard, T. J. 1990. "Angry Aggression Among the 'Truly' Disadvantaged." *Criminology* 28: 73–96.

Birkbeck, C., and G. LaFree. 1993. "The Situational Analysis of Crime and Deviance." *Annual Review of Sociology* 19: 113–37.

Black, D. J. 1993. *The Social Structure of Right and Wrong*. San Diego: Academic Press.

Black, D. 1983. "Crime as Social Control." *American Sociological Review* 48(1): 34–45.

Bureau of Justice Statistics. 1992. *Criminal Victimization in the United States: 1973–90 Trends*. (No. NCJ–139564). Washington, D.C.: U.S. Department of Justice.

Bursik, R. J. Jr., and H. G. Grasmick. 1993. *Neighborhoods and Crime: The Dimensions of Effective Community Control*. New York: Lexington Books.

Caputo, T., and C. Ryan. 1991. *The Police Response to Youth at Risk*. Ottawa: Solicitor General of Canada.

Cheatwood, D. 1996. "Interactional Patterns in Multiple Offender Homicides." *Justice Quarterly* 13(1): 107–28.

Christie, N. 1986. "Images of Man in Modern Penal Law." *Contemporary Crises* 10(1): 95–106.

Clarke, R. V. 1992. "Introduction." In R. V. Clarke, ed., *Situational Crime Prevention.* Albany, N.Y.: Harrow and Heston.

Cohen, L. E., and M. Felson. 1979. "Social Change and Crime Rate Trends: A Routine Activity Approach." *American Sociological Review* 44: 588–608.

Cornish, D. 1993. "Theories of Action in Criminology: Learning Theory and Rational Theory Approaches." In R. V. Clarke and M. Felson, eds., *Advances in Criminological Theory* (Vol. 5, pp. 351–82). New Brunswick, N.J.: Transaction.

Cox, B., and J. Collins. 1985. *Crime Victimization in the District of Columbia.* Research Triangle Park, N.C.: Research Triangle Institute.

Currie, E. 1985. *Confronting Crime.* New York: Pantheon Books.

Davis, P. W. 1991. "Stranger Intervention into Child Punishment in Public Places." *Social Problems* 38(2): 227–46.

Dixon, J., and A. Lizotte. 1987. "Gun Ownership and the Southern Subculture of Violence." *American Journal of Sociology* 93: 383–405.

Dollard, J. et al. 1939. *Frustration and Aggression: Theoretical and Empirical Reviews.* New Haven: Yale University Press.

Durkheim, E. 1964. *The Rules of Sociological Method.* New York: Free Press.

Eagly, A. H., and M. Crowley. 1986. "Gender and Helping Behavior: A Meta-Analytic Review of the Social Psychological Literature. *Psychological Bulletin* 100(3): 283–308.

Ellingworth, D., G. Farrell, and K. Pease 1995. "A Victim is a Victim is a Victim? Chronic Victimization in Four Sweeps of the British Crime Survey." *British Journal of Criminology* 35(3): 360–65.

Erlanger, H. S. 1975. "Is There a Subculture of Violence in the South?" *Journal of Criminology and Criminal Justice* 66 (December): 483–90.

Felson, M. 1994. *Crime in Everyday Life.* Newbury Park, Calif.: Pine Forge Press.

———. 1995. "Those Who Discourage Crime." In John E. Eck and David Weisburd, eds., *Crime and Place: Crime Prevention Studies* (Vol. 4, pp. 53–66). Monsey, N.Y.: Criminal Justice Press.

Felson, R. B., and H. J. Steadman. 1983. "Situational Factors in Disputes Leading to Criminal Violence." *Criminology* 21(1): 59–74.

Felstiner, W. 1974. "Influences of Social Organization on Dispute Processing." *Law and Society Review* 9: 63–94.

Felstiner, W. L. F., R. L. Abel, and A. Sarat. 1980–1981. "The Emergence and Transformation of Disputes: Naming, Blaming, and Claiming." *Law and Society Review* 15: 63–94.

Fischer, C. S. 1981. "The Private and Public Worlds of City Life." *American Sociological Review* 46 (June): 306–16.

Forde, D. R. 1992. "Survey Highlights." In *Winnipeg Area Survey Highlights* (No. 1, pp. 1–2). University of Manitoba: Winnipeg Area Study.

Forde, D. R., and L. W. Kennedy. 1997. "Risky Lifestyles, Routine Activities, and the General Theory of Crime." *Justice Quarterly* 14: 265–94.

Friedman, L. N., and S. B. Tucker. 1997. "Violence Prevention through Victim Assistance: Helping People Escape the Web of Violence." In R. C. Davis, A. J. Lurigio, and W. G. Skogan, eds., *Victims of Crime* (2d ed., pp. 183–93). Thousand Oaks, Calif.: Sage.

Gastil, R. D. 1971. "Homicide and a Regional Culture of Violence." *American Sociological Review* 36: 412–27.

Gelles, R. J., and M. A. Straus. 1988. *Intimate Violence.* New York : Simon and Schuster.

Gibbs, J. 1981. *Norms, Deviance, and Social Control: Conceptual Matters.* New York: Elsevier.

Gilligan, J. 1992. *Violence: Our Deadly Epidemic and Its Causes.* New York: Putnam.

Goffman, E. 1974. *Frame Analysis.* Garden City: Doubleday.

———. 1959. *The Presentation of Self in Everyday Life.* Garden City: Doubleday.

Gottfredson, M. R., and T. Hirschi. 1993. "A Control Theory Interpretation of Psychological Research on Aggression." In R. B. Felson and J. T. Tedeschi, eds., *Aggression and Violence: Social Interactionist Perspectives* (pp. 47–68.). Washington, D.C.: American Psychological Association.

———. 1990. *A General Theory of Crime.* Stanford, Calif.: Stanford University Press.

Grasmick, H. G. et al. 1993. "Testing the Core Empirical Implications of Gottfredson and Hirschi's General Theory of Crime." *Journal of Research in Crime and Delinquency* 30: 5–29.

Hackney, S. 1969. "Southern Violence." *American Historical Review* 74: 906–25.

Hagan, J., R. MacMillan, and B. Wheaton. 1996. "New Kid in Town: Social Capital and the Life Course Effects of Family Migration on Children." *American Sociological Review* 61(3): 368–85.

Hagedorn, J. 1994. "Homeboys, Dope Fiends, Legits, and New Jacks." *Criminology* 32, 2 (May): 197–220.

Hindelang, M. J., M. R. Gottfredson, and J. Garofalo. 1978. *Victims of Personal Crime: An Empirical Foundation for a Theory of Personal Victimization.* Cambridge, Mass.: Ballinger.

Hirschi, T. 1969. *Causes of Delinquency*. Berkeley: University of California Press.

Hirschi, T., and M. R. Gottfredson. 1993. "Commentary: Testing the General Theory of Crime." *Journal of Research in Crime and Delinquency* 30: 47–54.

———. 1994. "The Generality of Deviance." *Generality of Deviance* (pp. 1–22). New Brunswick, N.J.: Transaction.

Hocker, J. L., and W. W. Wilmot. 1985. *Interpersonal Conflict, 2d ed.* Dubuque, Iowa: Brown.

Hough, M. 1987. "Offenders' Choice of Target: Findings From Victim Surveys." *Journal of Quantitative Criminology* 3(4): 355–69.

Jencks, C. 1994. *The Homeless*. Boston: Harvard University Press.

Katz, J. 1988. *Seductions of Crime: Moral and Sensual Attractions in Doing Evil*. New York: Basic Books.

Keane, C., P. S. Maxim, and J. J. Teevan. 1993. "Drinking and Driving, Self-Control, and Gender: Testing a General Theory of Crime." *Journal of Research in Crime and Delinquency* 30(1): 3–29.

Kennedy, L. W. 1988. "Going it Alone: Unreported Crime and Individual Self-help." *Journal of Criminal Justice* 16(5): 403–12.

———. 1990. *On the Borders of Crime: Conflict Management and Criminology*. White Plains, N.Y.: Longman.

Kennedy, L. W., and D. R. Forde. 1996. "Pathways to Aggression: A Factorial Survey of 'Routine Conflict.'" *Journal of Quantitative Criminology* 12(4): 417–38.

———. 1990b. "Risky Lifestyles and Dangerous Results: Routine Activities and Exposure to Crime." *Sociology and Social Research* 74(3): 208–11.

———. 1990a. "Routine Activities and Crime: An Analysis of Victimization in Canada." *Criminology* 28(1): 137–52.

Kennedy, L. W., and R. A. Silverman. 1990. "The Elderly Victim of Homicide: An Application of Routine Activity Theory." *Sociological Quarterly* 31(2): 305–17.

Kennedy, L. W., R. A. Silverman, and D. R. Forde. 1991. "Homicide in Urban Canada: Testing the Impact of Economic Inequality and Social Disorganization." *Canadian Journal of Sociology* 16(4): 397–410.

Kennedy, L. W., and S. W. Baron. 1993. "Routine Activities and a Subculture of Violence: A Study of Violence on the Street." *Journal of Research in Crime and Delinquency* 30(1): 88–112.

Kleck, G. 1996. "Crime, Culture Conflict, and the Sources of Support for Gun Control." *American Behavioral Scientist* 39(4): 387–404.

———. 1991. *Point Blank: Guns and Violence in America.* New York: A. de Gruyter.

Kleck, G., and M. DeLone. 1993. "Victim Resistance and Offender Weapon Effects in Robbery." *Journal of Quantitative Criminology* 9(1): 55–81.

Kleck, G., and S. Sayles. 1990. "Rape and Resistance." *Social Problems* 37(2): 149–62.

Kornhauser, R. 1978. *Social Sources of Delinquency.* Chicago: University of Chicago Press.

Latane, B., and S. Nida. 1981. "Ten Years of Research on Group Size and Helping." *Psychological Bulletin* 89(2): 308–24.

Laub, J. H., and R. J. Sampson. 1993. "Turning Points in the Life Course: Why Change Matters to the Study of Crime." *Criminology* 31: 301–26.

Lavrakas, P. J. 1993. *Telephone Survey Methods: Sampling, Selection, and Supervision.* Newbury Park, Calif.: Sage.

Luckenbill, D. 1977. "Criminal Homicide As a Situated Transaction." *Social Problems* 25(2): 176–86.

Luckenbill, D., and D. P. Doyle. 1989. "Structural Position and Violence: Developing A Cultural Explanation." *Criminology* 27: 419–36.

Lynch, J. P. 1987. "Routine Activity Theory and Victimization at Work." *Journal of Quantitative Criminology* 3(4): 283–300.

Lynch, J. P., and M. Danner. 1993. "Offense Seriousness Scaling: An Alternative to Scenario Methods." *Journal of Quantitative Criminology* 9: 309–22.

Mather, L., and B. Yngvesson. 1980–1981. "Language, Audience, and the Transformation of Disputes." *Law and Society Review* 15: 775–822.

McClintock, F. H. 1970. "The Dark Figure." *Collected Studies in Criminological Research* (pp. 13–27, 31–34). Strasbourg: Council of Europe.

McGuire, K., A. L. Pastore, and T. J. Flanagan, eds. 1995. *Sourcebook of Criminal Justice Statistics.* Washington, D.C.: U.S. Department of Justice.

Meier, R. F., and T. D. Miethe. 1993. "Understanding Theories of Criminal Victimization." In *Crime and Justice* (Vol. 17, pp. 459–499).

Menard, S. 1995. *Applied Logistic Regression Analysis.* Thousand Oaks, Ca.: Sage.

Merry, S., and S. Silbey. 1984. "What Do Plaintiffs Want? Reexamining the Concept of Disputes." *Justice System Journal* 9(2): 151–78.

Messner, S. 1982. "Societal Development, Social Inequality and Homicide: A Cross-National Test of a Durkheimian Model." *Social Forces* 61: 225–40.

Miethe T. D., and R. F. Meier. 1994. *Crime and its Social Context: Toward an Integrated Theory of Offenders, Victims, and Situations*. Albany, N.Y.: State University of New York Press.

Miethe, T. D., M. C. Stafford, and J. S. Long. 1987. "Routine Activities/Lifestyle and Victimization." *American Sociological Review* 52: 184–94.

Miller, N. 1990. "Valid Theory-Testing Meta-Analyses Further Question the Negative State Relief Model of Helping." *Psychological Bulletin* 107(2): 215.

Minerbrook, S. 1994. "A Generation of Stone Killers." *US News and World Report*, pp. 33–37.

National Institute of Justice. 1996. *The Cycle of Violence Revisited* (Research Preview). Washington, D.C.: National Institute of Justice.

Nelsen, C., J. Corzine, and L. Huff-Corzine. 1994. "The Violent West Reexamined: A Research Note on Regional Homicide Rates." *Criminology* 32: 149–61.

Newman, O. 1972. *Defensible Space: Crime Prevention through Urban Design*. New York: Macmillan.

Nossiter, A. April 1996. "Goetz Ordered to Pay $43 Million to Paralyzed Victim." *Miami Herald*, p. 1.

Polk, K. 1995. "Lethal Violence As a Form of Masculine Conflict Resolution." *The Australian & New Zealand Journal of Criminology* 28(1): 92–115.

Reiss, A., and J. A. Roth. 1993. *Understanding and Preventing Violence*. Washington, D.C.: National Academy Press.

Roncek, D. W., and M. A. Pravatiner. 1989. "Additional Evidence that Taverns Enhance Nearby Crime." *Sociology and Social Research* 73(4): 185–88.

Ross, J. I. 1995. "A Process Model of Public Police Violence." *Criminal Justice Policy Review* 7(1): 67–90.

Rossi, P., and S. L. Nock. 1982. *Measuring Social Judgments*. Beverly Hills, Calif.: Sage.

Sacco, V. F., and H. Johnson. 1990. *Patterns of Criminal Victimization in Canada*. Ottawa: Minister of Supply and Services.

Sacco, V. F., and L.W. Kennedy. 1996. *The Criminal Event: An Introduction to Criminology*. Belmont, Calif.: Wadsworth.

Sampson, R. J., and J. Laub. 1993. *Crime in the Making: Pathways and Turning Points Through Life*. Cambridge, Mass.: Harvard University Press.

Sataline, S. January 1994. "Teen Struggles to Come to Terms with Death Row: Florida Man Awaits Execution for '92 Murder, Committed at 16." *The Buffalo News*, p. 6.

Savitz, L., K. Kumar, and M. Zahn. 1991. "Quantifying Luckenbill." *Deviant Behavior* 12(1): 19–29.

Shaw, C. R., and H. D. McKay. 1942. *Juvenile Delinquency in Urban Areas*. Chicago: University of Chicago Press.

Sherman, L., P. Gartin, and M. Buerger. 1989. "Hot Spots of Predatory Crime: Routine Activities and the Criminology of Place." *Criminology* 27(1): 27–55.

Shotland, R. L., and M. K. Straw. 1976. "Bystander Response to an Assault: When a Man Attacks a Woman." *Journal of Personality and Social Psychology* 34: 990–99.

Silbey, S., and A. Sarat. 1987. "Critical Traditions in Law and Society Research." *Law and Society Review* 21(1): 165–74.

Silverman, R. A., and L. W. Kennedy. 1993. *Deadly Deeds: Murder in Canada*. Toronto: Nelson.

Skogan, W. G. 1984. "Reporting Crimes to the Police: The Status of World Research." *Journal of Research in Crime and Delinquency* 21: 113–37.

Stoddart, K. 1981. "As Long As I Can't See You Do It: A Case Study of Drug-Related Activities in Public Places." *Canadian Journal of Criminology* 23(4): 391–405.

Straus, M. 1985. *The Index of Legitimate Violence*. Unpublished manuscript, Family Research Lab. Durham: University of New Hampshire.

Sykes, G., and D. Matza. 1957. "Techniques of Neutralization: A Theory of Delinquency." *American Sociological Review* 22: 664–70.

Tedeschi, J. T., and R. B. Felson. 1994. *Violence, Aggression, and Coercive Actions*. Washington, D.C.: American Psychological Association.

Thompson, W. E. 1986. "Courtship Violence: Toward a Conceptual Understanding." *Youth and Society* 18(2): 162–76.

Tremblay, R. E. et al. 1996. "Do Canadian Children Become More Aggressive as They Approach Adolescence?" In *Growing Up in Canada (Report on the National Longitudinal Survey of Children and Youth)*, pp. 127–38. Ottawa: Government of Canada.

Van Brunschot, E. 1996. *The Assault Event: Individuals, Interactions, and Interpretations*. Unpublished doctoral dissertation. Alberta: University of Alberta.

Widom, C. S. 1989. "The Cycle of Violence." *Science* 244: 160–66.

———. 1995. *Victims of Childhood Sexual Abuse—Later Criminal Consequences*. (Report No. NCJ 151525). Washington, D.C.: National Institute of Justice.

Wilson, J. Q. 1994. "What to do About Crime." *Commentary* (September): 25–34.

Wilson, J. Q., and R. J. Herrnstein. 1985. *Crime and Human Nature.* New York: Simon and Schuster.

Wilson, W. J. 1991. "Studying Inner-City Social Dislocations: The Challenge of Public Agenda Research." *American Sociological Review* 56 (February): 1–14.

Wolfgang, M., and F. Ferracuti. 1967. *The Subculture of Violence.* London: Social Science Paperbacks.

Zillman, D. 1988. "Cognitive-Excitation Interdependencies in Aggressive Behavior." *Aggressive Behavior* 14(1): 51–64.

———. 1983. "Transfer of Excitation in Emotional Behavior." In J. T. P. Cacciopo, and R. E. Petty, *Psychophysiology* (pp. 215–40). New York: Guilford Press.

Subject Index

Author Index